What You ... Are Saying

I strongly recommend that educators interested in high-quality discussion as both a form and outcome of pedagogy read *Civil Discourse: Classroom Conversations for Stronger Communities.* Schmidt and Pinkney bring decades of experience to the task of expertly situating the need to teach young people how to participate in civil discourse in our current political context. Through lively and well-written narrative, the authors bring a lot of new wine to a venerable bottle. Readers will walk away with strong rationales for focusing on civil discourse in schools, along with very clear and pragmatic examples of what good looks like.

—Diana E. Hess
Dean
University of Wisconsin–Madison School of Education

How can schools and teachers prepare our youngest citizens to actively engage in discourse about issues in society? Schmidt and Pinkney's book brilliantly explains why discussing contentious issues matters, for both the future of our democracy and student learning, while providing a wealth of practical ideas and resources for teachers. This book couldn't be more timely and enduring.

—Stefanie Rosenberg Wager
Past President of the National Council for the Social Studies

Helping young people to learn to discuss contentious issues is one of the most promising ways to strengthen—and even to save—our republic. In *Civil Discourse: Classroom Conversations for Stronger Communities*, Schmidt and Pinkney provide a scholarly, thoughtful, and also highly practical guide to doing just that. Teachers will find it extraordinarily useful.

—Peter Levine
Tisch College of Civic Life
Tufts University

Schmidt and Pinkney are seasoned and masterful social studies educators and advocates. They present the topic of civil discourse in a manner that is knowledgeable and approachable. The strategies presented in *Civil Discourse: Classroom Conversations for Stronger Communities* implore educators to be courageous and incorporate these techniques and practices in their classrooms.

—**Amber Coleman-Mortley**
Podcaster, Civic Evangelist, and Parent Educator

Masterful and timely, Schmidt and Pinkney's *Civil Discourse: Classroom Conversations for Stronger Communities*, is—to paraphrase David McCullough—"a guide [for social studies teachers] to navigation in perilous times." This brilliantly scaffolded set of practices guides social studies teachers through the often-challenging process of bringing meaningful and constructive civil discourse into the classroom. This is a must-have for your social studies classroom.

—**Nathan McAlister**
Social Studies Teacher
2010 National History Teacher of the Year

Schools can never be culturally neutral terrains devoid of politics. And because of this, educators will continue to grapple with the teaching of potentially contentious topics. We live in a time where students and educators are confronted with political debates, blatant racism, a global pandemic, and more. *Civil Discourse* offers classroom teachers and school leaders a practical guide to facilitate classroom conversations with knowledge and sensitivity. It will equip you with strategies and tools to not only act tomorrow but to critically reflect on your own practice as an educator.

—**Darnell Fine**
Instructional Coach

Civil discourse is essential for a functioning democracy. Schmidt and Pinkney lay out a step-by-step guide using building blocks that allow educators to help build communities in their classrooms by allowing them to foster civil discourse with their students. They involve multiple stakeholders in the solution-based approach to discussing contentious topics in classrooms and how that can make a larger impact outside the classroom. This is a must-read for all who work with students and who want to make an impact through civil discourse.

—**Elizabeth Evans**
Director of Civic Education
Center for Political Thought and Leadership
Arizona State University

Civil Discourse: Classroom Conversations for Stronger Communities offers hope and help for educators during this highly polarized moment. Co-authors Schmidt and Pinkney urge educators to take courage and view contentious topics as an opportunity to train and instill understanding, belonging, and empathy in students. This book is packed with ideas, tips, and strategies to aid the educator in successfully establishing and cultivating a classroom where civil discourse leads to a community where students learn to accept and celebrate differences with maturity and respect; with *Civil Discourse*, students will learn how to think, not what to think.

—Karalee Wong Nakatsuka
United States History Teacher
Arcadia, CA
2019 Gilder Lehrman California History Teacher of the Year

Engaging students in discussion requires the teacher to think about much more than which questions to ask. Covering everything from how to communicate with parents to what to do when discussions go awry, this succinct guide provides educators with the foundations and strategies they need to create high-quality classroom discussions.

—Paula McAvoy
PhD Coordinator for the Social Studies Program Area of Study
North Carolina State University

Now, more than ever, our young people need to be equipped with the right tools to engage in critical conversations that will allow them to take informed action on issues that negatively impact our society. *Civil Discourse*, with its practical guidance for building community, cultivating empathy, and leaning into discomfort with contentious topics, is exactly the type of resource that educators, no matter the subject area, need to support the next generation of change makers. Bravo and thank you!

—Fay Gore
Former Director of K–12 Social Studies,
North Carolina Department of Public Instruction
Co-Editor of the *College, Career, and Civic Life (C3) Framework for Social Studies State Standards* (2013)

In a time of increasing political and social polarization, understanding the ins and outs of civil discourse has never been more important or potentially more impactful. As with so much else, it is often left up to our educators to navigate a difficult path in ensuring that students learn how to engage in civil discourse around difficult conversations. *Civil Discourse: Classroom Conversations for Stronger Communities* provides both experienced and beginning educators with a way to navigate that path. It is an engaging and enjoyable map for the educator looking for a way forward in improving discussion and tackling tough issues!

—Steve Masyada
Executive Director
Lou Frey Institute
University of Central Florida

This is a timely and needed work for teachers engaging in democratic education. The authors both provide practical approaches to engaging with controversies within the classroom and take on key issues of the day—namely, polarization, the effects of misinformation, and the need to engage with others in civil and empathic ways. They make the case for how schools can play a role in addressing these issues and provide practical and applicable steps forward for teachers at a time when these practices may place them under a political microscope in their communities.

—Jeremy Stoddard
Professor of Curriculum and Instruction
Director of Graduate Studies and UW Teach
University of Wisconsin–Madison

Schmidt and Pinkney write at a time when the need for students to engage in true dialogue and discourse is more important than ever. The pointed examples, protocols and structures, and compelling data make this an essential tool for every educator who engages in such rich topics. Students are naturally curious, opinionated, and eager to discuss bold ideas and controversial concepts, and as a result, they need deft educators who are equipped to teach the skills in discourse while thinking critically, suspending judgement. This book fills an important void in the education of educators to effectively nurture a community of learners, of any age, to critically explore the ideas, beliefs, and perspectives of those around them.

—Scott Thomas
Minnesota School Administrator

Schmidt and Pinkney have created a road map for educators to build confidence in instilling the skills of civic engagement in students. As they brilliantly note, by not talking to those with whom we disagree, we are choosing to ignore our interdependence. Economic, social, educational, and environmental benefits can all develop in the form of a well-informed voter focused not on the correct answer but rather on the correct way to navigate civil discourse. This reading gives me hope that students today will be better equipped to create a sustainable civil society for us all.

—Stephanie Rogers Canter
EdTech Professional, Advocate for Progressive
Educational Policy, and Local Elected Official

I can almost hear social studies teachers' collective sigh of relief. Schmidt and Pinkney have written a book that illuminates one of education's great challenges and offers realistic, reasonable, and attainable recommendations. The balance of structure and flexibility in their approach reflects an authentic understanding of what it means to be a classroom teacher in this moment. The authors honor teachers' professionalism and expertise, with vigorous assurance that we all have much to learn. The whole book feels like a PLC of gifted, welcoming teachers gathered in a comfortable teachers' lounge, coffee in hand, ready to solve all the world's problems.

—Jessica Ellison
Teacher Education and Curriculum Development
Minnesota Historical Society

Schmidt and Pinkney indisputably define and provide a road map/strategy for civil discourse. In a time when barbershop, hair salon, club, and church meeting conversations can turn contentious and even violent at times, these strategies are a welcomed resource. Providing our students with the necessary skills and processes of considerate, thought-provoking discourse may foster transformation of our individual communities.

—Chanda Robinson
CEO and Founder
Chanda Robinson Consulting
Member of the National Council for the
Social Studies Board of Directors

Schmidt and Pinkney provide a blueprint for teachers who face the daily challenge of tackling contentious topics. *Civil Discourse: Classroom Conversations for Stronger Communities* is a timely resource that will assist teachers with building a classroom culture built on courage, understanding, belonging, and empathy. Teachers are provided helpful strategies that will bolster teacher confidence and ultimately make a positive impact on student learning.

—Daniel Kelley
Principal
Smithfield High School
Smithfield, RI

With our homogenized neighborhoods and echo chamber media bubbles, schools are one of the few places where Americans can engage in discourse about important topics with people who hold differing viewpoints. *Civil Discourse* provides teachers with clear guidance on how to facilitate these invaluable conversations in their classrooms. Teachers from all grade levels will benefit from the wisdom found in these pages.

—Bruce Lesh
Former High School Teacher and Social
Studies Department Chair, Baltimore County Public Schools

Learning how to teach contentious issues is difficult for preservice teachers who don't yet have the confidence to facilitate these types of discussions with students. *Civil Discourse: Classroom Conversations for Stronger Communities* is a road map for teachers on how to get started. Schmidt and Pinkney focus on building community, which is often overlooked in conversations about teaching contentious topics. They lay a foundation for how to have civil discourse in all classrooms—not just social studies ones. This book highlights civil discourse as a life skill—one that all teachers can practice learning from.

—Annie McMahon Whitlock
Associate Professor of Elementary Education
University of Michigan-Flint

In a time when a primer on engaging students in meaningful and purposeful discourse on public matters has never been more needed, Schmidt and Pinkney deliver a comprehensive vision. Each chapter provides a substantive explanation and actionable recommendations for how teachers, collaborative teams, and administrations can work to transform social studies instruction into a much needed foundry for democratic citizenship.

—Jenifer Hitchcock
Teacher
Thomas Jefferson High School for Science and Technology

It's time we stop talking about creating active and knowledgeable citizens and start the actual process of training our students to engage in civil and civic discourse. One reason we often push this process to the back burner in our lesson plan books is because we're just not sure what that can look like. In *Civil Discourse: Classroom Conversations for Stronger Communities*, Schmidt and Pinkney provide not just a powerful rationale for developing engaged citizens but the practical tools to make it happen. If you're like me and are tired of randomly searching online for how to facilitate difficult but absolutely vital conversations, then *Civil Discourse* was written specifically for you. Schmidt and Pinkney provide the structure, strategies, and resources you're looking for and that your students need. A perfectly timed book for every educator!

—Glenn Wiebe
Curriculum Consultant

This is a must-have book for every educator's personal library. Schmidt and Pinkney provide an invaluable framework and "how-to" guide for teachers who want to foster healthy civil discussions on controversial issues. The authors make this difficult pedagogical task accomplishable, and their practical guidance strengthens the ability of schools to succeed in their most important mission of developing young people into empathetic, informed, and active citizens.

—Brian Brady
Founder and President
Youth Engage

Civil Discourse: Classroom Conversations for Stronger Communities provides teachers with a step-by-step practical framework on how to engage students in civil discourse. The framework allows teachers to fully implement the civil discourse framework or make adjustments to their current instructional practices. I really appreciate the discussion on the differences between debate, discussion, and dialogue to ensure that students and teachers learn the differences between the concepts and help students engage in meaningful conversations about American politics.

—Averill Kelley
Social Studies Teacher
Holmes Scholar and PhD Candidate at University of Nevada

Schmidt and Pinkney's book is a wonderful primer for educators who need a jumpstart or a refresher on discourse in civics education. They have gathered many practical and useful tips, guides, and resources for the classroom and personal edification for beginning and veteran educators alike. This book is a must-have for anyone teaching in the social studies classroom and training future social studies educators. As a classroom guide and when designing curriculum, Schmidt and Pinkney's book is an invaluable tool for working with students to create strong and engaging discourse civics education.

—Melissa R. Collum
Teaching Professional
Viterbo University

How will students practice and master the skills of engaging in challenging discussions with people of diverse viewpoints if those conversations aren't happening in classrooms? While the past few years have seen a rise in resources aimed at convincing teachers of this need, too few offer a road map to help make this happen. *Civil Discourse* offers the classroom teacher a step-by-step approach to fostering productive civic dialogue in their classroom. Each chapter identifies a list of essential teacher practices and action steps a teacher can take to make those practices their own. This book is a valuable resource for teachers and teacher-educators looking to bring meaningful discussion back into classrooms.

—Shannon Salter Burghardt
Founding Teacher
Building 21 Allentown

Civil Discourse

From Joe:

This book is dedicated to Donald Henry Schmidt, Jr.

You are the greatest man I have ever known.

I am lucky to have you as my dad.

I love you.

From Nichelle:

This book is dedicated to Michelle Burmah-Jones and John Pinkney

for always pushing me to do better and letting me know I had a voice.

Civil Discourse

Classroom Conversations for Stronger Communities

Joe Schmidt

Nichelle Pinkney

CORWIN

CORWIN
A SAGE Publishing Company

FOR INFORMATION:

Corwin
A SAGE Company
2455 Teller Road
Thousand Oaks, California 91320
(800) 233-9936
www.corwin.com

SAGE Publications Ltd.
1 Oliver's Yard
55 City Road
London EC1Y 1SP
United Kingdom

SAGE Publications India Pvt. Ltd.
B 1/I 1 Mohan Cooperative Industrial Area
Mathura Road, New Delhi 110 044
India

SAGE Publications Asia-Pacific Pte. Ltd.
18 Cross Street #10-10/11/12
China Square Central
Singapore 048423

Printed in the United States of America

Library of Congress Cataloging-in-Publication Data

Names: Schmidt, Joe, author. | Pinkney, Nichelle, author.

Title: Civil discourse : classroom conversations for stronger communities / Joe Schmidt, Nichelle Pinkney.

Description: Thousand Oaks, California : Corwin, 2022. | Series: Corwin teaching essentials | Includes bibliographical references and index.

Identifiers: LCCN 2021059383 | ISBN 9781071856192 (paperback) | ISBN 9781071876961 (epub) | ISBN 9781071876985 (epub) | ISBN 9781071876992 (pdf)

Subjects: LCSH: Community and school—United States. | School environment—United States. | Classroom environment—United States. | Civics—Study and teaching—United States.

Classification: LCC LC221 .S268 2022 | DDC 371.19—dc23/eng/20220302
LC record available at https://lccn.loc.gov/2021059383

This book is printed on acid-free paper.

President: Mike Soules
Vice President and Editorial Director: Monica Eckman
Executive Editor: Tori Mello Bachman
Acquiring and Content Development Editor: Sharon Wu
Editorial Assistant: Nancy Chung
Project Editor: Amy Schroller
Copy Editor: Christina West
Typesetter: C&M Digitals (P) Ltd.
Cover Designer: Gail Buschman
Marketing Manager: Margaret O'Connor
Editorial Consultant: Julie Stern

23 24 25 26 10 9 8 7 6 5 4 3 2

Contents

online resources

For additional resources related to *Civil Discourse*, please visit the companion website at **resources.corwin.com/civildiscourse.**

Acknowledgments

First and foremost, Joe and Nichelle would like to thank Julie Stern for serving as our author mentor. You took on the challenge of writing this book with us and never stopped smiling and being there for us. Also, we give a big thank you to Sharon Wu, Tori Bachman, Nancy Chung, and everyone at Corwin who believed in us and allowed us to make our dreams a reality.

We also want to thank all of the educators who are working with students to engage in civil discourse and the administrators and community members who support the educators. Without your passion, none of this would be possible.

From Joe:

This book could not have happened without the support of my friends and family who lost me to countless hours of reading and writing. I would like to give a special thank you to my wife, Peggy, for always helping me to remember to live in the present tense and to my daughter, Honore, who always serves as my first editor.

Thank you also to Keith Long and Dan Kallgren for inspiring my love of social studies that started my path in education and to Deb Foster and Jesse Bradley for helping me get my footing during the early years of my career. To Norma Furger, Denise Kalscheur, Tamara Maxwell, and the entire

MMSD Literacy team, thank you for helping me find my voice. I can never say thank you enough to Kris McDaniel for taking the time to mentor me until I finally started to believe in myself. To my colleagues Stefanie Wager, Scott Abbott, Steve Maysada, and all of CS4, thank you for being the support group I never knew I needed. Thank you Jeff Maves, Shane Gower, David Greenham, Janette Kirk, Lee Anne Larsen, the Secondary SIS team, and the iCivics Educator Network for your friendship and patience during this project while always being there to serve as a thought partner and helping make sure I never lose sight of what is going on in our classrooms and communities. Thank you to Dr. Diana Hess, Dr. Paula McAvoy, and Dr. Peter Levine for your tireless efforts and research, which have served as the inspiration for much of this work.

Lastly, thank you Nichelle Pinkney for taking this journey with me. To learn from you and work with you as we breathed life into these pages was a life-changing experience. I could not have done it alone and I will always value our newfound friendship!

From Nichelle:

This labor of love became a reality because of divine intervention and Twitter. I am so thankful to my amazing co-author, Joe Schmidt, for choosing me to go on this journey with him. I have learned and grown so much; this is just the beginning, my friend!

To my amazing siblings for being my first students even when they didn't want to, thank you. I also thank my nieces and nephews for their willingness to sacrifice their "nana time" so I could meet my deadlines. And to the thousands of students who helped me grow to be the teacher I am today, this book would not have been possible without my days on 3443 Fannett Road on D hall.

Thank you to all the amazing teachers that I have worked with, coached, and mentored. There's nothing like being on teams that push you to grow. To my LTT team, thank you for encouraging me and being that support system.

Lastly, to Sheliah Moss, my ninth-grade U.S. History teacher: Thank you for telling me I was a LEADER and that I could change the world. You held me to this as a student, a team member, and then when I became your department chair 10 years later. Because of your words and faith in me, I strive to build leaders in every student and teacher I interact with. Ms. Moss, you were RIGHT . . . I am a LEADER, I will be heard . . . I am now one step closer to changing the world we live in.

PUBLISHER'S ACKNOWLEDGMENTS

Corwin gratefully acknowledges the contributions of the following reviewers:

Valencia Abbott
History/Social Studies Teacher
Rockingham County Schools and Sankofa Consulting

Juan Carmona
Teacher and Dual Enrollment Instructor
Donna High School and South Texas College

Tinisha Shaw
Social Studies Teacher, SEL Specialist, and Instructional Coach
Guilford County Schools

About the Authors

Joe Schmidt has worked as a high school teacher and college professor for elementary preservice teachers, and he has also held roles in district and state-level leadership in support of both rural and urban schools. Throughout his career, Joe has served in a variety of leadership positions with numerous social studies–related organizations across the United States that align with his passion for supporting inspiring and impactful educational opportunities for both students and educators.

Nichelle Pinkney has been a social studies educator for the past 16 years, working as a classroom teacher to a K–12 curriculum director. She has presented and trained teachers nationally and internationally. Nichelle holds a masters of art in educational administration from Lamar University and a bachelor's degree in sociology with a minor in women's studies from Salem College. Nichelle has found passion in providing equitable education to every student. She has worked to revise curriculum to ensure that it is diverse, equitable, and inclusive for all students and teachers.

Introduction

Civil Discourse Strengthens Communities

> *There is no power for change greater than a community discovering what it cares about.*
>
> Margaret Wheatley

We are at a crossroads as individual nations and as a global community. Political polarization is on the rise and every decision seems to become a flashpoint of anger and resentment (Dimok & Wike, 2020; Lutz Fernandez, 2021). But it doesn't have to be this way. In fact, many studies find that people agree more on local politics than national politics, where organized forces such as political parties telling us what to believe have less influence on our opinions (Jensen et al., 2021). And successful conflict-resolution programs have shown dramatic results in fostering discourse even after violent conflict (North, 2003; Steele, 2021).

The two of us—Joe Schmidt and Nichelle Pinkney—are social studies educators who see civil discourse as the key component to building community. We wrote this book to help educators leverage opportunities to examine our differences in a way to strengthen all of us. As American writer Audre Lorde (1984) wrote, "It is not our differences that divide us. It is our inability to recognize, accept, and celebrate those differences." This book is a first step for educators who recognize the value of discussing contentious topics. We develop an understanding of each other through engaging in civil discourse, which allows for the accepting and celebrating of our inevitable differences.

With experience as a classroom teacher in both high school and college as well as roles in district and state-level leadership, Joe has a combination of classroom experience as well as big-picture thinking done in support of educators in both rural and urban districts. He has also served in a variety of positions with social studies–related organizations across the United States, which have provided insight into how to make connections between resources available for educators and how to best implement those resources in the classroom with students. Joe's professional network allows him to collaborate with educators who represent the diverse perspectives and issues that we see in schools today. He sees student conversations as one of the most important and engaging parts of a student's education and always encourages his students to have an opinion, even if that opinion may be subject to change as students continue to learn more about the topic.

Nichelle Pinkney's life experiences as a woman of color teaching and leading social studies education in the southern United States has given her insight into the importance of navigating contentious topics with careful planning and clear communication. She regularly writes lesson plans and assessments for all courses and grade levels from kindergarten through high school and conducts professional development to help teachers improve their craft. She seeks to empower teachers to move past the fear that has become a common part of their jobs by giving them tools to prepare students for democratic participation in a diverse, pluralistic society.

Even though we both have backgrounds in social studies, the need for civil discourse transcends the lines of content areas. Throughout this book, you will see examples related to non–social studies classes as well as ideas, suggestions, and frameworks that are applicable in almost every classroom. By the end, we hope that districts use this book to create curriculum and policy that supports all students and all educators in all content areas, because we are all a part of something bigger than a single subject area and classroom.

Every person on Earth belongs to distinct communities, and individuals depend on these communities for survival and for living meaningful lives. A community is simply a group of people living in the same place or having a particular characteristic in common. We are a part of several communities in our lifetimes that help to establish and formulate who we are and who we are destined to become. Infants have both an innate need and desire to belong to a community. In the school system, we establish the importance of belonging to a community as early as kindergarten. We teach the characteristics of a strong community and how to maintain them in the walls of the school, with the hope that this will eventually permeate the cities and countries we live in.

When people come together in communities, disagreement is inevitable. We all disagree with our friends and family on simple things like where to go for dinner or who is responsible for cleaning the kitchen. Part of maturity and strong self-development requires us to listen, empathize, seek understanding, and even compromise. The trouble is, with contentious topics, we often resort to one of two poor choices: avoidance or fighting.

But there is a better way. Civil discourse is an alternative to either avoidance or fighting, as shown in Figure 0.1. The building blocks of civil discourse are courage, understanding, belonging, and empathy. This book helps educators build these foundations so that students learn the skills necessary to navigate thorny issues with maturity and respect for those who hold differing opinions.

Through our communities, we learn how to come together even when it is uncomfortable. As history has shown,

FIGURE 0.1 The Spectrum of Contentious Topics

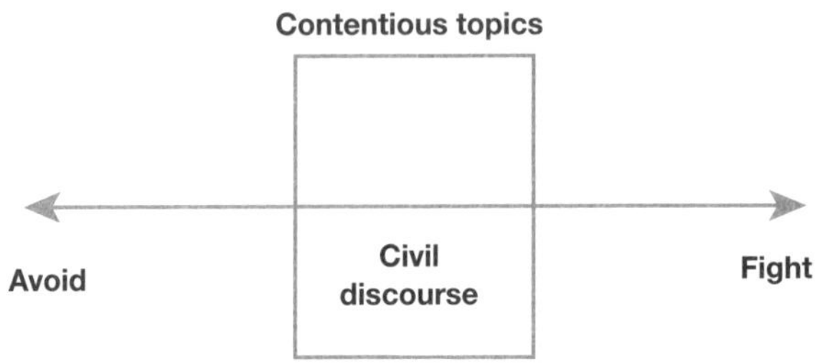

sometimes we get this right and sometimes we do not. Imagine if the following topics were avoided rather than brought out for formal discussion. When the need arises, we have to be courageous in discussing contentious topics for the betterment of our communities.

Consider these examples:

- In the 1840s, at a time when strong customs and beliefs held that women should be subservient to men in all aspects of life, a community of both women and men came together to discuss the social, civil, and religious condition and rights of women. Through shared discourse about many contentious aspects of the topic, this community of people wrote the Declaration of Sentiments and their efforts would eventually lead to the passage of the 19th Amendment granting women the right to vote in the United States.
- During the extreme discrimination, oppression, and violence against African Americans in the 1950s, tensions ran high even among those who sought to change these circumstances. Disagreements among activists threatened to derail their mission. But disciplined discourse led to specific messaging for different groups, a result of practicing empathy, and bolstered the organization and tactics of the U.S. Civil Rights Movement.

- At the end of the Cold War, thousands of nuclear weapons were in danger of theft and deployment by nefarious groups. The Cooperative Threat Reduction program, which was responsible for the safe destruction of thousands of nuclear weapons, was the result of years of careful discourse and negotiations (Shonk, 2019).
- In the 1990s, members of the law enforcement community teamed up with the broadcasting community to formally discuss ways to save children from abduction. The conclusion of that discourse is now known as the AMBER Alert, which broadcasts a serious—and uncomfortable—topic across television and radio stations when a child is reported missing. The program has now expanded to cell phone users and to date, over 600 children across the United States have been saved as a result.

In all of these monumental historical examples, there are four common themes that arise: courage, shared understanding, belonging, and empathy. This book is organized by these themes, with each chapter providing resources for educators to teach the skills of discourse to their students. We cannot simply walk into a classroom and ask students to discuss abortion or gun control, for instance, without adequate planning and preparation. We have to gradually lead up to this type of discourse. Chapter 5 is where we offer distinct strategies, but recognize that the first four building blocks must be laid before we get there.

Chapter 1 focuses on the **courage** to embrace our discomfort and come together as a group because it is the first step toward establishing strong communities. As psychologist Susan David (2017) says, "Discomfort is the price of admission to a meaningful life." Many of us prefer to avoid difficult or sticky conversations, choosing to ignore them and hoping they will go away, but that is the exact opposite of what strong communities need. When we avoid tough conversations, we weaken our civil societies and make ourselves vulnerable to the power hungry.

The next building block is shared **understanding**, especially around key terms, which we focus on in Chapter 2. We have to be sure that the words we use have the same meaning to all members of the discourse community. And when we shift the focus toward understanding rather than "winning," we can help our young people have productive conversations that are sorely needed in today's divided society.

Although communities are essential for human survival, we want to do more than survive. We want to thrive, and a strong sense of **belonging** is the next piece of the puzzle for strong communities, which is the focus of Chapter 3. Healthy communities acknowledge that each member belongs in their community, even when those members have differing thoughts, views, cultures, and abilities. Educators can set up their classroom communities to foster this sense of belonging that is so essential to living meaningful lives.

Finally, strong communities practice **empathy**, recognizing that each member has a unique and valid perspective, which is the focus of Chapter 4. By viewing the world through other people's perspective, we can better understand each other and live together in harmony. Strong communities thrive on the concepts of embracing and acknowledging courage, common good, belonging, and empathy of their members. This book seeks to build these values back into our school communities.

With that foundation in place, we can have **discourse** around contentious topics, which is the focus of Chapter 5. To help busy educators remember these building blocks, we can use the acronym **CUBED**. This book sets the foundation for discourse through fostering courage, understanding, belonging, and empathy that leads to productive discourse for stronger communities. Each chapter provides a checklist at the end to ensure teachers are prepared to foster civil discourse with their students. See Figure 0.2 for our visual of the building blocks of discourse.

Schools play an essential role in our communities. As we type this, there are hurricanes, wildfires, and floods gripping the United States and many other parts of the world. We face a climate crisis, a physical and mental health crisis, a global refugee and migration crisis, and the backsliding of democracies across the globe. While it is certainly not the job of students or teachers to solve these challenges, we can build an important foundation by equipping young people with strong skills in discourse around contentious topics. If we get this right, we have the chance to emerge stronger than ever. Thank you for joining us.

FIGURE 0.2 Building Blocks of Discourse

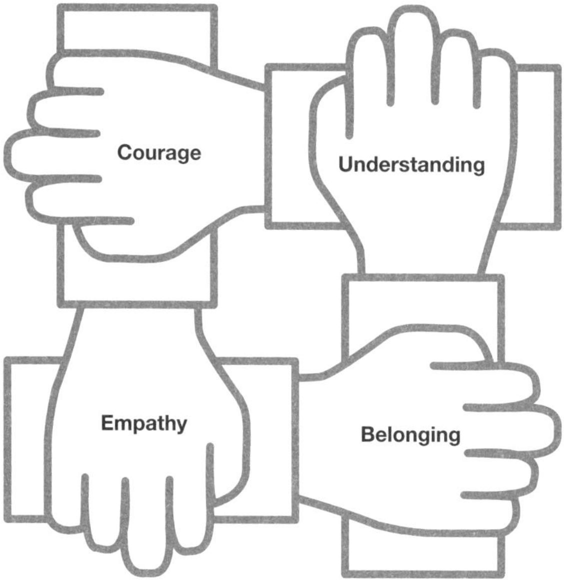

CHAPTER 1

Courage

Why Discomfort Can No Longer Be Avoided

It's uncomfortable to challenge the status quo. It's uncomfortable to resist the urge to settle. When you identify the discomfort, you've found the place where a leader is needed. If you're not uncomfortable in your work as a leader, it's almost certain you're not reaching your potential as a leader.

—Seth Godin (2009)

This chapter will help to prepare you to complete the following:

- ✓ Find connections in your school or district mission or vision statements that support students engaging in civil discourse.
- ✓ In partnership with administrators, develop a vision statement for social studies education in your school or district that highlights the importance of civil discourse.
- ✓ Set parameters around which topics are open for discourse.
- ✓ Communicate the vision statement to parents and the larger community.

MODERN SOCIETY AND THE THREAT TO DEMOCRACY

Are you ready to get uncomfortable? This question is usually met with a "no" or with awkward silence. In an age where everything is about catering to our comfort, why would we seek to be uncomfortable? On the one hand, avoiding discomfort is part of living an easy life. On the other hand, avoiding discomfort around questions of how we participate in society, function in our community, and interact with others causes problems larger than our own levels of comfort.

Take a moment and reflect on the following questions:

- Has the search for our own personal comfort delivered us to a place where we no longer feel like we can meaningfully participate in our society?
- Do we now live in isolated bubbles separate from those who traditionally would have benefited from us and those we would have benefited from?
- As we become more and more isolated in our own personal search for comfort, what parts of our community and society suffer?
- What parts of our lives suffer when our own search for comfort means that we lash out at other people in our lives who disagree with us so that we might protect the beliefs and ideas that bring us comfort?
- Are we ready to step into the discomfort and be the leader that our students need right now?

If we cannot talk to those with whom we disagree, then we are choosing to cut off parts of our lives and ignore our common humanity and interdependence. In his book, *Bowling Alone: The Collapse and Revival of American Community* (2000), Robert Putnam posits that among the biggest factors in the decline of civic involvement of Americans is decreasing attendance in community organizations, groups, and clubs. Without participation in these groups, we have lost what connects individuals of differing political backgrounds and beliefs. Calls for schools to prepare students to be civically active have grown more urgent in recent decades because schools have increasingly become one of the few shared spaces left in our society.

Since the release of *Bowling Alone*, we have seen increased access to the internet and cable television and, more recently, the rise of social media. These forms of communication have made it easier to find those who agree, regardless of where we might live. We are now better able to avoid discomfort by avoiding those who may disagree with us and by finding more people who agree with us. This creates a confirmation bubble to stay comfortable in. Comfortable, that is, until we are forced to cross paths with someone who does disagree with us. This is where social media has become the new town square that allows for soapbox speeches of competing ideas minus many of the social norms that govern how we converse and interact.

Social media has exacerbated differences in opinion and made us more likely to argue with someone we know or even someone we don't know. Most people are now familiar with the term "internet trolls" and many of us have firsthand experience with what some will say online when they can hide behind anonymity. Traditional social norms have not fully evolved in the age of social media.

Without these norms, social media has become a place where we exchange insults instead of ideas and real relationships are impacted by the words exchanged through a screen. In 2017, the Pew Research Center reported that 4 in 10 Americans had personally experienced online harassment and 95% of Americans said that people being harassed or bullied online is a problem (Figures 1.1 and 1.2, respectively) (Duggan, 2017). These are factors that resulted in 27% of Americans choosing not to post something online after seeing how others were treated (Figure 1.3) (Duggan, 2017).

FIGURE 1.1 Percentage of Americans Who Have Experienced Online Harassment

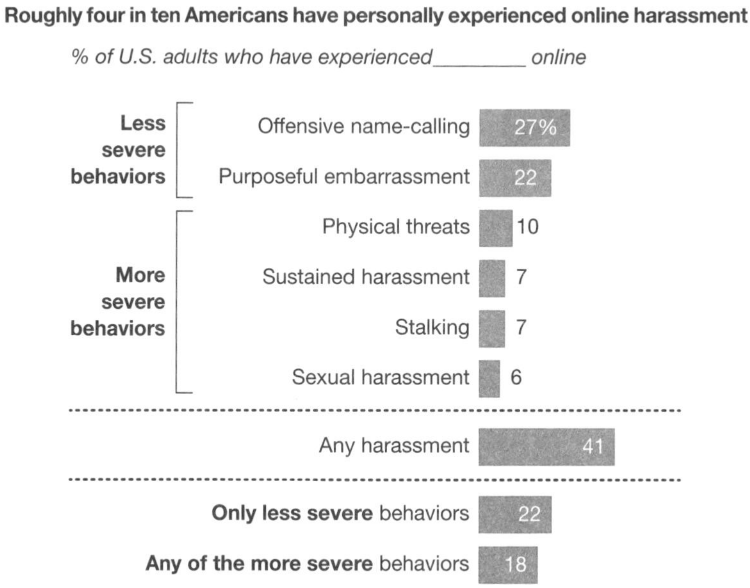

SOURCES: Survey conducted Jan. 9–23, 2017. "Online Harassment 2017." Pew Research Center.

Duggan (2017).

Online harassment is negatively impacting the lives of people, as this is where a lot of us now spend our time interacting with one another. In our work with people across the United States and even internationally, we ask people if they had enough practice in contentious conversations in their K–12 educational experience. The consensus from everyone we meet is that our students could use more practice in disagreeing respectfully and with maturity. In fact, many adults need to develop these skills as well.

Citizen University (2021), a 501(c)(3) nonprofit organization, envisions "a great civic revival across our nation—our dream is a country in which Americans are steeped in a sense of civic character, educated in the tools of civic power, and are

FIGURE 1.2 Percentage of Americans Who Identify Online Harassment or Bullying as a Problem

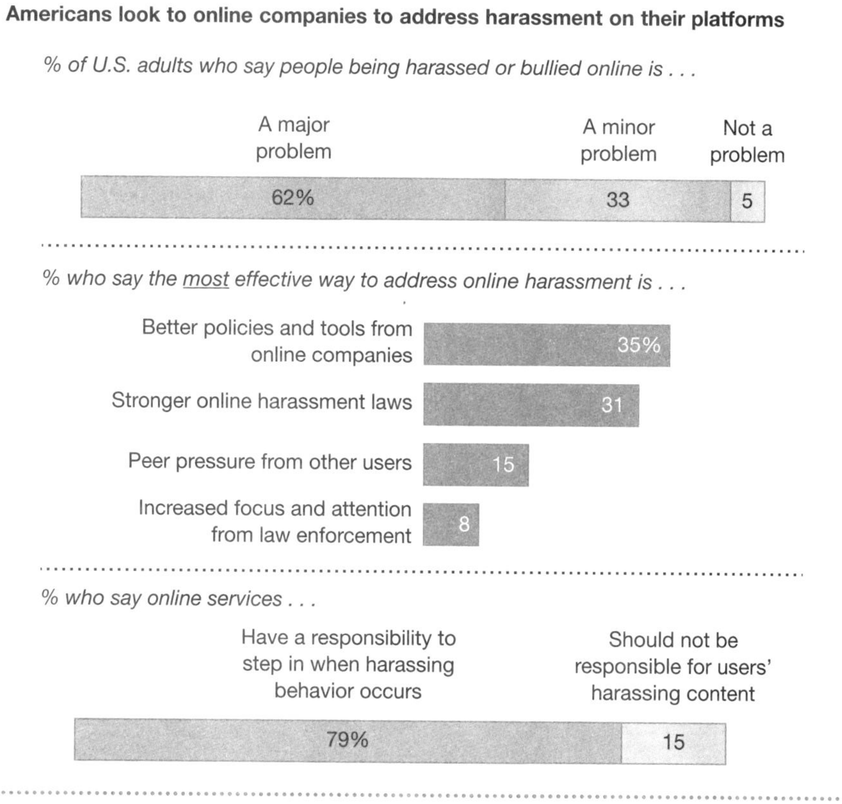

SOURCES: Survey conducted Jan. 9–23, 2017. "Online Harassment 2017." Pew Research Center. Duggan (2017).

problem-solving contributors in a self-governing community." To achieve this, they "design gatherings, rituals, and workshops that focus on civic power and civic character as the building blocks of powerful citizenship." Among these are their Civic Saturday events where people gather to participate in what they call a "civic sermon."

Civic Saturdays allow for both "friends and strangers to nurture a shared purpose in our democracy" (Citizen University,

FIGURE 1.3 Percentage of Americans Who Choose Not to Post Something Online Based on How Others Are Treated

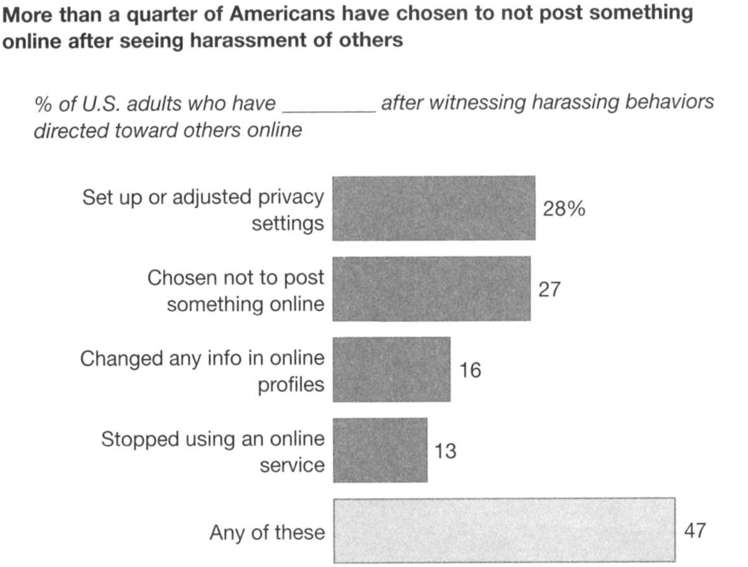

SOURCES: Survey conducted Jan. 9–23, 2017. "Online Harassment 2017." Pew Research Center.

Duggan (2017).

NOTE: Total may not add to 100% because respondents could select multiple options.

2021). The shared purpose is developed through the discussion of ideas across the political spectrum. Eric Liu (2019), cofounder and CEO of Citizen University, talks about the power of attending a Civic Saturday in his TED Talk, "How to Revive Your Belief in Democracy":

> When you come to a Civic Saturday and are invited to discuss a question like "Who are you responsible for?" or "What are you willing to risk or to give up for your community?" When that happens, something moves. You are moved. You start telling your story.

> We start actually seeing one another. You realize that homelessness, gun violence, gentrification, terrible traffic, mistrust of newcomers, fake news—these things aren't someone else's problem; they are the aggregation of your own habits and omissions. Society becomes how you behave.

What are the habits and omissions that Liu is referring to? Are they the same habits that we have developed to protect our own comfort? When we withdraw from our communities because we do not feel comfortable in disagreeing with someone else, does our omission perpetuate a society in which the ability to disagree with someone is not valued? If society becomes how we behave, then withdrawing to our own personal comfort level at the expense of interacting with others leads to the rationale of withdrawing while still not understanding that our own withdrawal contributes to the problem.

Dr. Peter Levine (2013), Associate Dean of Tisch College of Civic Life at Tufts University, highlights the importance of citizenship in his book, *We Are the Ones We Have Been Waiting For*. Working backward, Levine tells us that in order to achieve social justice, good government and strong communities are essential. In order to have good government and strong communities, we must have active citizenship from members of our society. During a speech at the Frontiers of Democracy Conference, Levine (2014) defined citizenship as "deliberation + collaboration + civic relationships." All three components involve interacting with as opposed to withdrawing from others.

Leaving the comfort of our self-imposed bubbles is essential to the work of maintaining our communities. A community relies on the ability of people to deliberate in order to determine the best course of action, collaborate in order to put the idea into action, and develop civic relationships in order to keep moving ideas forward (Dusso & Kennedy, 2015). The importance of this cannot be understated, as "large amounts of the deliberation, collaboration, and civic relationships actually do pay off in terms of economic, social, educational, environmental benefits" (Levine, 2014). Overcoming our fear of discomfort in order to actively engage with others through deliberation and collaboration is required to sustain and strengthen our communities.

THE ROLE OF SCHOOLS

John F. Kennedy famously asked, "If not us, who? If not now, when?" This is the same question facing educators in our world today. Educators live at a unique intersection of being adults living in the present as well as working with the students who will become the adults of tomorrow. With the great privilege of seeing into the future, educators also carry the burden of being able to influence that future. Historian and journalist Henry Adams once said, "A teacher affects eternity; he can never tell where his influence stops."

A civic revival is the cure to a world of online harassment and growing societal isolation. This revival must have roots in the classrooms of today in order to be sustainable. If the cure to what ails us is not in the hands of educators teaching students to engage in civil discourse, then who holds the key? If now is not the time to take up these conversations, then when will be the right time for our schools to lead?

Social studies educators look at the world with a lens that asks, "How would I teach this in my classroom?" Our world is one of uncomfortable topics and a society struggling to address them. To maintain our comfort, we avoid talking about these topics or we talk without truly listening to others. If we do not listen, then we do not have to face the reality that others might not agree with us or, even worse, that our beliefs may be misguided or incorrect. But what about our students in our schools? Should our students expect to learn in spaces where discomfort is avoided at all times?

Among the general public, one common fear or misunderstanding is that a curriculum tells students what beliefs they should walk away with. But that is not the purpose of a curriculum. Nor should educators push their own beliefs onto their students. The goal of a classroom is to create a curriculum and a learning environment where students feel comfortable practicing the skills of discourse with their peers around topics with which they may not agree, with the teacher acting as a skilled facilitator and model of courage and maturity.

While educators should remain neutral facilitators, students actually enjoy hearing diverse views from their classmates. The work of Dr. Diana Hess and Dr. Paula McAvoy sheds light on the impact of sharing differing opinions with one another:

> Students would report that in discussions where there was a lot of shared opinion, those were not as interesting as in discussions where there were differing views . . . They were really responding to the fact that it's quite interesting to hear what your peers think about things. And not just that they have different points of view but what they're supporting those points of view with. (Drummond, 2015)

Moreover, discomfort lies at the heart of *all* learning and growth. Many educators are familiar with the work of Lev Vygotsky. His work around the zone of proximal development focuses on student learning outside of the comfort zone of what they already know (Vygotsky, 1978). The idea is that we intentionally move students beyond what they can comfortably do by providing them guidance and support from a "more knowledgeable other," as shown in Figure 1.4. This may be a teacher or a peer providing the necessary support, but the essential component to student learning is moving students outside of their comfort zone. We cannot allow our students to avoid discomfort in our classrooms if we want them to learn.

Schools should not reflect society's tendency to shy away from tough topics. Schools should lead the way by providing students with a safe space to be uncomfortable. Educators should model the skills of active listening, considering multiple points of view, determining the reliability of evidence, and yes, even sharing a bit about how their thinking has changed or evolved after gaining more insight, with topics that are not as contentious so as to remain relatively neutral on those.

FIGURE 1.4 Zone of Proximal Development

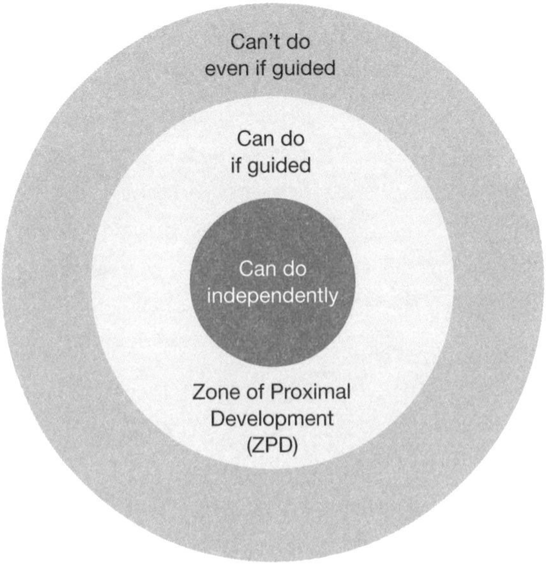

Acknowledging that differences in opinions may divide us, the introduction to the College, Career, & Civic Life (C3) Framework for Social Studies State Standards highlights that despite these differences, we do share universal goals for social studies education:

> Advocates of citizenship education cross the political spectrum, but they are bound by a common belief that our democratic republic will not sustain unless students are aware of their changing cultural and physical environments; the past; read, write, and think deeply; and act in ways that promote the common good. There will always be differing perspectives on these objectives. The goal of knowledgeable, thinking, and active citizens, however, is universal. (National Council for the Social Studies, 2018)

The contemporary issues of today are often rooted in ideas that have been disagreed about for decades if not centuries. To learn our history with a depth of understanding, students have to face the realities of living in a country that continues to struggle with these contentious ideas. How do we teach these familiar histories while also giving these stories context, meaning, and connection to the present day?

What is your comfort level in leading a student discussion about these topics?

- Politics and elections
- Racial issues and inequities
- Economic policies and how they impact different people
- Gender rights
- Constitutional rights
- Religious beliefs and protections

- Upholding individual rights while looking out for the common good
- Celebrating diversity while also promoting unity
- Treating people fairly versus treating people equally
- Following laws that conflict with one's moral ethics
- Interacting with our physical world and natural resources

A lot of these topics are becoming hot-button issues that cause problems for educators, even when handled in a manner that allows for open, thoughtful discourse. None of those topics call out a specific contentious issue; rather, they encompass overarching concepts that span across content areas. We need to provide the context to practice the skills of civil discourse if we are to support our students in becoming knowledgeable, thinking, and active citizens.

Creating active citizens is often a reason we are called to be social studies teachers, and it is a democratic imperative. This responsibility is one of the most consistent ideals that has been expressed throughout the modern history of education in the United States. Back in 1848, Horace Mann warned,

> But to avoid such a catastrophe, shall all teaching, relative to the nature of our government, be banished from our schools; and shall our children be permitted to grow up in complete ignorance of the political history of their country? In the schools of a republic, shall the children be left without any distinct knowledge of the nature of a republican government; or only with such knowledge as they may pick up from angry political discussions, or from party newspapers; from caucus speeches, or Fourth of July orations—the Apocrypha of Apocrypha?

Even then, educational leaders were worried about students getting caught up in the rhetoric of angry politics!

While the divided political scene of today is a fresh concern in our minds, remember that Horace Mann had similar worries back in 1848. Mann said education would provide the information students needed to know about their government as opposed to what they might hear as part of angry political discussions. Almost two centuries later, Dr. Diana Hess implored teachers to have their students lean into these heated disagreements as part of their learning: "Part of our job is to teach young people how to talk with one another, especially with people who have differing views" (Van Benthuysen & Hodgin, 2019).

Influential education reformer John Dewey (1934) took Mann one step further as he addressed the role of our students in society as a whole: "The purpose of education has always been to every one, in essence, the same—to give the young the things they need in order to develop in an orderly, sequential way into members of society." Horace Mann focused on supporting the republic, but John Dewey believed an orderly society to be the responsibility of schools and the primary purpose of education (EdSource, 2002).

In January 1957, the ASCD (Association of Supervision and Curriculum Development) Committee on Platform of Beliefs combined the ideas of schools supporting the republic and students becoming members of society: "The main purpose of the American school is to provide for the fullest possible development of each learner for living morally, creatively, and productively in a democratic society" (ASCD, 2012). According to ASCD, it was not enough for students to be able to function in both our society and in our republic. Schools needed to bring students to their "fullest possible development" in support of these goals.

ASCD is not alone in their belief in schools to produce students capable of critical thinking and engaged citizenship. In "The Curriculum Matrix: Transcendence and Mathematics," Arthur W. Foshay (1991) saw a vision of education to produce fully developed human beings: "The one continuing purpose of education, since ancient times, has been to bring people to as full a realization as possible of what it is to be a human being" (p. 277). With an emphasis in recent years of teaching to the whole child, Foshay tells us that this should be and always has been the goal of education for our students.

Having students discuss problematic issues is not something to be done only in social studies classrooms; rather, this type of engaged learning should be at the heart of a child's education. By the start of the 21st century, connections were made between character education and the role of schools in engaging students in real-life problem-solving. Schaps et al. (2001) identified schools as the place where this type of learning could properly happen for young people:

> The best forms of character education are those that enlist students as active, influential participants in creating a caring and just environment in the classroom and in the school at large . . . The challenge is for the school to become a microcosm in which students practice age-appropriate versions of the roles they must face in later life—and deal with the related problems and complications.

So if these essential skills are no longer practiced in normal, everyday life, then where can we reasonably expect these skills to be practiced? As one of the few shared spaces left in our communities, it is becoming increasingly important that schools are able to take the lead on developing the citizens who will both lead and participate in all facets of our communities in the future. This is not a responsibility that schools can afford to turn away from. In her book *Controversy in the Classroom: The Democratic Power of Discussion*, Dr. Hess (2009) explains why this is an obligation of our schools:

> [S]chools have not just the right, but also the obligation, to create an atmosphere of intellectual

> and political freedom that uses genuine public controversies to help students discuss and envision political possibilities. Addressing public controversies in schools not only is more educative than quashing or ignoring differences, it also enhances the quality of decision-making by ensuring that multiple and competing views about controversial political issues are aired, fairly considered, and critically evaluated. (p. 6)

Hess is not alone in the idea that schools are the correct and essential place to work on these skills. Dr. Peter Levine identifies three essential things that schools should be doing in order to prepare students for meaningful civic participation (Arizona State University, 2020). One of these is to "learn how to deliberate matters of disagreement with other people." Levine argues that not only is school a place to learn this, but that schools are a *better* place to learn these skills. Learning how to deliberate matters of disagreement with other people is a "question of both skills and knowledge" that can be practiced and should be taught (Arizona State University, 2020). The idea that these are skills that need to be taught almost demands that schools be the place where students practice these skills alongside the content knowledge necessary to engage in thoughtful discourse. With guidance, discussions can be grounded in information as well as emotions and rhetoric.

There is a misleading idea that schools are preparing students for the "real world." Perhaps this is partially true, but with smartphones, social media, and the internet, there is no longer a strict divide between the lives of our students while they are in school and the real world outside of school. When it comes to the ability to engage in civil discourse in order to share ideas and express opinions, the real world is only a click or an app away. We can no longer reasonably expect to shield our students from the responsibilities of adulthood when some of our students are already expanding their worlds in ways we could have never imagined. Schools have to be a safe place to practice the skills of disagreement and discomfort, because the digital world often is not a safe space for real discourse. We owe it to our students to prepare them for life outside of school.

As technology increases the availability of primary sources available to the general public, the classroom use of primary sources has accelerated as well. As Dr. Sam Wineburg noted in a 2018 interview with *Perspectives on History*, "This device [his cellphone] is in many ways more powerful than any library we have had from 1900 to 1970" (Elliott, 2018). While access to information has become easier, so has access to misinformation that muddies the waters. Access to information has changed so rapidly that our media literacy skills have not been able to keep up. As we have opened the door to focusing on more and multiple perspectives, we have also unlatched the gate to information that is dubious at best and outright lies at worst.

Society in general and students in particular have struggled to understand what is reliable and what is useful only in reinforcing our own beliefs. Figure 1.5 presents the results of a Stanford History Education Group (2019) survey on student mastery of civic online reasoning. Even as high school students get better each year at "going online and discerning fact from fiction," all data points are below a 40% success rate, with more than half of the categories in single digits.

While many of us will agree with the earlier quote that our smartphones are "more powerful than any library," it must be noted that the process of being published and included in a library was and is far more rigorous than the current process of posting information online.

FIGURE 1.5 Percentage of Students Scoring Emerging or Mastery on Civic Online Reasoning by Grade and Task

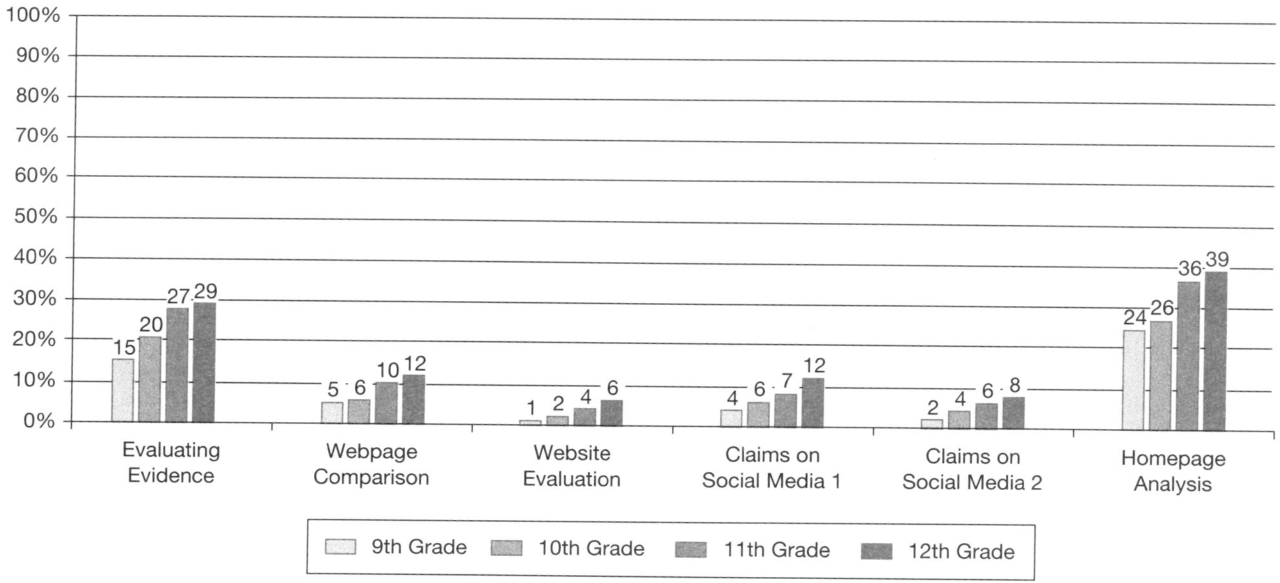

SOURCE: Stanford History Education Group (2019).

NOTE: This figure includes 2939 students who selected a grade category although the number of responding students varied by task. Excluded categories include "8th grade" and "missing."

> What once fell on the shoulders of editors, fact-checkers, and subject matter experts now falls on the shoulders of each and every one of us. But there's a problem with this new reality. As the journalist John H. McManus reminds us, in a democracy the ill-informed hold just as much power in the ballot box as the well-informed. The future of the republic hangs in the balance. (Wineburg, 2015, p. 16)

Although educators may hesitate to let their students engage in research on the internet, we must never lose sight of the importance of reinforcing our students' ability to reach reasoned conclusions. This means they must be able to state a claim, provide evidence, and explain the reasoning that connects the evidence to their claim across all content areas.

Having students understand that there are multiple ways to approach an idea, concept, or problem is one of the deeper learning transferable skills that many educators strive for as they dig into the content of their classroom. Rote memorization has made way for the practical application of skills that relies on a student's ability to process content information to potentially reach multiple acceptable answers or potential solutions to a problem.

In the title of his book, *Why Won't You Just Tell Us the Answer?* Bruce Lesh (2011) sums up the struggles that students may have with this shift. We cannot blame our students for having this mindset of strictly looking for the correct answer. Our students have come of age in a school system that stresses correct answers as opposed to correct thinking. The 21st-century school requires students to step out of their comfort zone of always looking for the correct answer. Instead we need to engage them in a dialogue that reflects their thinking beyond a single story.

The focus of social studies education and history education in particular has been moving toward the notion of not focusing on a single right answer. Instead we want to reinforce the use and development of skills that support the processing of information in order to reach a well-reasoned response. This means that schools have seen a shift in pedagogy away from the memorization of names, dates, and places and in its place, movement toward a classroom environment where students are doing the work that historians themselves would do. Students are now engaging in historical inquiry with the goal of corroborating information to reach plausible and defensible answers given the information at hand.

CONCRETE STEPS FOR EDUCATORS

Now that we have established the need for educators to engage students in civil discourse, how do we do it in a way that minimizes conflict, missteps, and upset? This section outlines four concrete steps for teachers to take to create the first building block of courage to foster civil discourse.

1. Align to school mission or vision statements.
2. Create a social studies vision statement.
3. Set broad parameters on topics.
4. Communicate with parents and the larger community.

First, review the big-picture goals of your school or district to find alignment to civil discourse. These provide a shared language and agreed-upon goals from which to begin your planning and preparations. Many large districts have recently adopted a portrait of a graduate or a learner profile. Consider these examples from one of the largest school districts in the United States:

- Employs active listening strategies to advance understanding.
- Respects divergent thinking to engage others in thoughtful discussion.

- Demonstrates the ability to work interdependently within a group to promote learning, increase productivity, and achieve common goals.
- Analyzes and constructs arguments and positions to ensure examination of a full range of viewpoints.
- Acknowledges and understands diverse perspectives and cultures when considering local, national, and world issues.
- Contributes to solutions that benefit the broader community.
- Demonstrates empathy, compassion, and respect for others.
- Acts responsibly and ethically to build trust and lead. (Fairfax County Public Schools, 2014)

Starting here puts everyone on the same page for what we are trying to achieve. Use these as a starting point and schedule a meeting with your direct supervisor or social studies department at your school or district to discuss the next step.

Second, in collaboration with your supervisor and administration, craft a short vision statement for social studies that is aligned to what you've discovered in the school vision or mission statement. For instance, the National Council for the Social Studies (2010) states, "The primary purpose of social studies is to help young people make informed and reasoned decisions for the public good as citizens of a culturally diverse, democratic society in an interdependent world." A statement like this can be used when communicating to parents in step 4, such as posting it on the class web page, school newsletter, course outline or syllabus, and even in social studies classrooms.

Third, articulate clear guardrails on how to determine which topics or perspectives are open for examination and which ones are not. For instance, a school district in Texas issued a clarifying statement when one of its senior administrators suggested that elementary teachers have books on "opposing views" of the Holocaust (Killough, 2021). This example points to the need to clarify two types of questions: open versus settled.

In her book *Controversy in the Classroom*, Hess (2009) introduces us to what she identifies as the importance in differentiating between what she calls "open" versus "settled" questions. Open questions are those that experts in the field are actively working to answer, such as the most effective economic policies to reduce inequality or poverty. Settled questions are those that the vast majority of the expert community accept as the empirical evidence that answers the question.

For instance, the question of whether or not the Earth is warming has overwhelming empirical data affirming this truth, yet the idea of global warming is a contentious one for many people. Similarly, questions related to vaccines and their related health impacts have been repeatedly proven with scientific research and data, yet those who disagree with these findings are often significant voices in the public debate on the safety of vaccines.

Schools can offer clarity that says we don't discuss every contentious topic found on social media. We discuss topics that are open, political questions of which there is a lack of consensus among the expert community on the answer. Award-winning history teacher Ayo Magwood explained what open versus settled or closed questions look like in her classroom:

> Open means it is still up for debate, closed means that a vast majority of the social scientists on this issue agree on a conclusion. So we don't discuss closed issues in the classroom. We don't discuss whether the Holocaust existed. We do not discuss whether vaccines create autism, because there is a discoverable answer and it has been discovered. (Stern & Aleo, 2020)

Magwood goes on to explain that she begins conversations about race in the United States with empirical data. Are there empirical data that show that race plays a role in people's lives? Yes. This can be seen in Pew Research Center (2016) data on unemployment (Figure 1.6), income (Figure 1.7), education (Figure 1.8), home ownership (Figure 1.9), and court and prison systems (Figure 1.10). Magwood communicates to her students, administration, and students' parents that the question of whether or not systemic racism exists is settled and therefore not discussed as a topic to examine from multiple perspectives. "But *what to do about* systemic racism is

FIGURE 1.6 Race and Unemployment

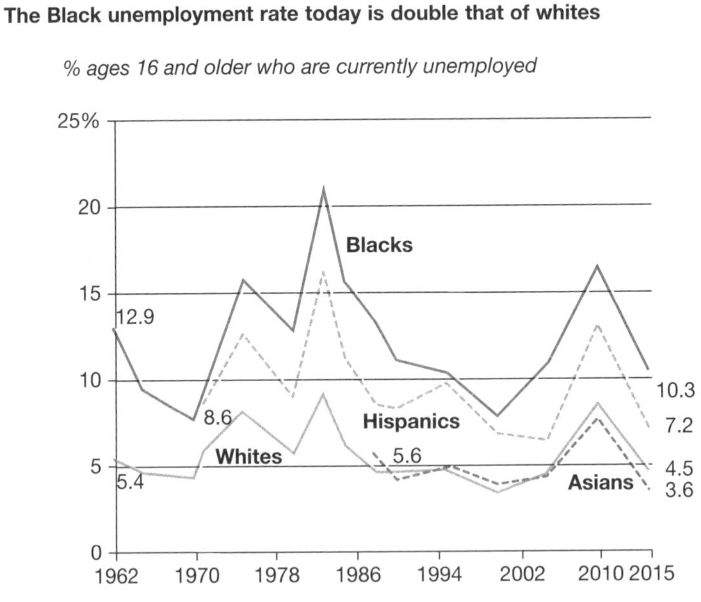

SOURCES: Pew Research Center tabulations of the 1962–2015 Current Population Survey Annual Social and Economic Supplement (IPUMS).

"On Views of Race and Inequality, Blacks and Whites Are Worlds Apart."

Pew Research Center (2016).

NOTE: The unemployment rate refers to the share of the labor force (those working or actively seeking work) who are not employed. Whites, Blacks and Asians include only those who reported a single race. Native Americans and mixed-race groups not shown. Data for whites, Blacks and Asians from 1971 to 2015 include only non-Hispanics. Data for whites and Blacks prior to 1971 include Hispanics. Data for Hispanics not available prior to 1971. Hispanics are of any race. Data for Asians not available prior to 1988. Asians include Pacific Islanders.

FIGURE 1.7 Race and Household Income

Racial gaps in household income persist

Median adjusted household income in 2014 dollars

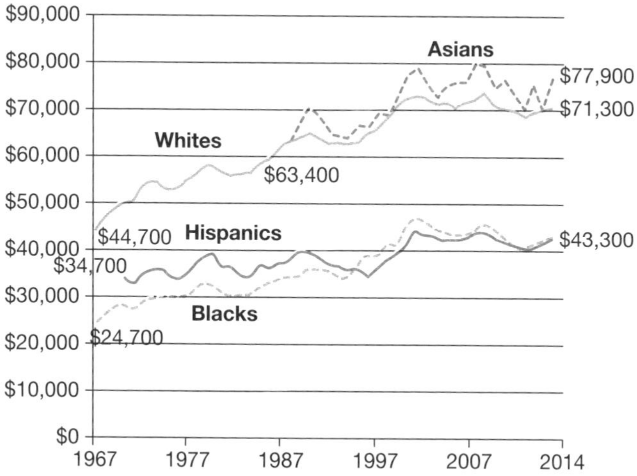

SOURCES: Pew Research Center tabulations of the 1968–2015 Current Population Survey Annual Social and Economic Supplement (IPUMS).

"On Views of Race and Inequality, Blacks and Whites Are Worlds Apart."

Pew Research Center (2016).

NOTE: Income standardized to a household size of three and is reported for the calendar year prior to the survey year. For details, see Methodology. Race and ethnicity are based upon the race and ethnicity of the head of household. Whites, Blacks and Asians include only those who reported a single race. Native Americans and mixed-race groups not shown. Data for whites, Blacks and Asians from 1970 to 2014 include only non-Hispanics. Data for whites and Blacks prior to 1970 include Hispanics. Data for Hispanics not available prior to 1970. Data for Asians not available prior to 1987. Asians include Pacific Islanders.

certainly an open, political question, and that we *will* discuss and consider from multiple perspectives," says Magwood.

This is the same for many of the contentious topics that our society is currently wrestling with. We shouldn't be asking, "Is the climate changing?" but rather, "What should we do about it?" Religion, guns, crime, drugs, immigration, health care, and many more contentious topics are closely connected to how people view themselves as human beings. Therefore,

FIGURE 1.8 Race and Higher Education

Whites are more likely than Blacks to have college degree

% of U.S. adults ages 25 and older who have at least a bachelor's degree

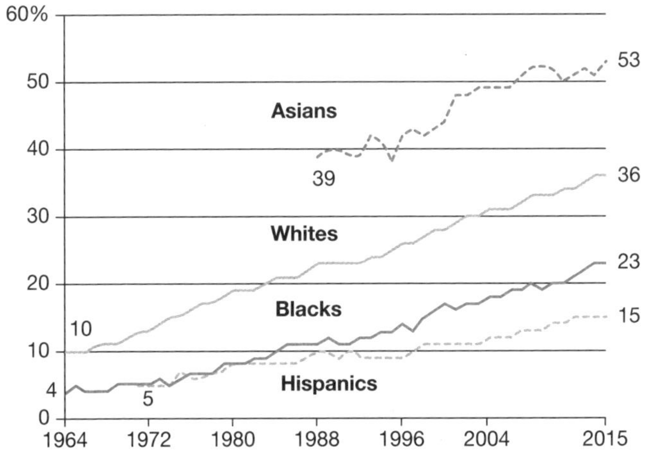

SOURCES: Pew Research Center tabulation of the 1964–2015 Current Population Survey Annual Social and Economic Supplement (IPUMS).

"On Views of Race and Inequality, Blacks and Whites Are Worlds Apart."

Pew Research Center (2016).

NOTE: Whites, Blacks and Asians include only those who reported a single race. Native Americans and mixed-race groups not shown. Data for whites, Blacks and Asians from 1971 to 2015 include only non-Hispanics. Data for whites and Blacks prior to 1971 include Hispanics. Data for Hispanics not available prior to 1971. Hispanics are of any race. Data for Asians not available prior to 1988. Asians include Pacific Islanders. Prior to 1992 those who completed at least 16 years of school are classified as having a bachelor's degree.

we first address the empirical data available to agree upon what we know definitively. Then we turn our attention to discussing the best solutions for how society should handle our differences in opinions instead of our opinions of people. The skills needed in these conversations are skills that can be practiced in our classrooms.

Dr. Wineburg's (2010) research supports this view on the importance of evidence to offer credibility to ideas. He says, " . . . while everyone is entitled to an opinion, not every opinion deserves to be believed. In history, a persuasive opinion is

FIGURE 1.9 Race and Home Ownership

Homeownership is more common among whites than other racial and ethnic groups

% of ___ householders owning a home

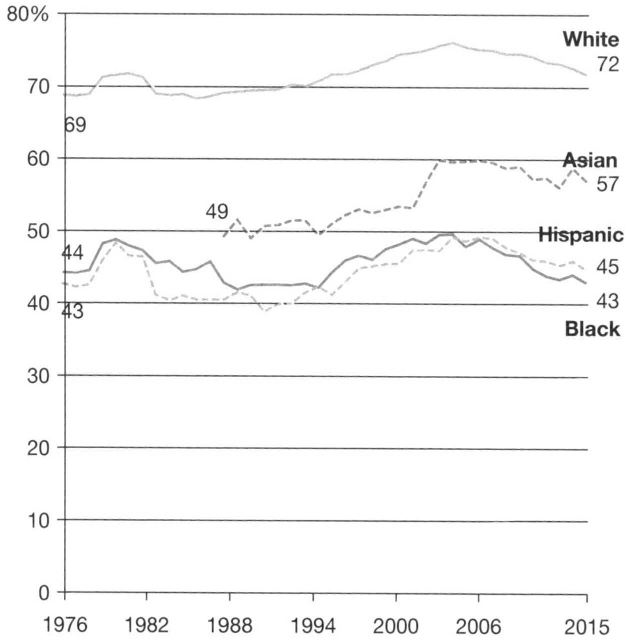

SOURCES: Pew Research Center tabulations of the 1976–2015 Current Population Survey Annual Social and Economic Supplement (IPUMS).

"On Views of Race and Inequality, Blacks and Whites Are Worlds Apart."

Pew Research Center (2016).

NOTE: Race and ethnicity based on the race and ethnicity of the head of household. White, Black and Asian householders include only non-Hispanics who reported a single race. Native Americans and mixed-race groups not shown. Data for Asians not available prior to 1988. Asians include Pacific Islanders. Hispanics are of any race.

one backed up by evidence" (p. 2; McManus, 2012). Claims, evidence, and reasoning are essential skills in all subject areas. More specifically in social studies, this means the ability of students to engage in historical thinking to properly source, contextualize, and corroborate the evidence as part of a close read (Stanford History Education Group, 2020).

FIGURE 1.10 Race and Imprisonment Rates

Imprisonment rates have declined across racial and ethnic groups—especially among Black Americans

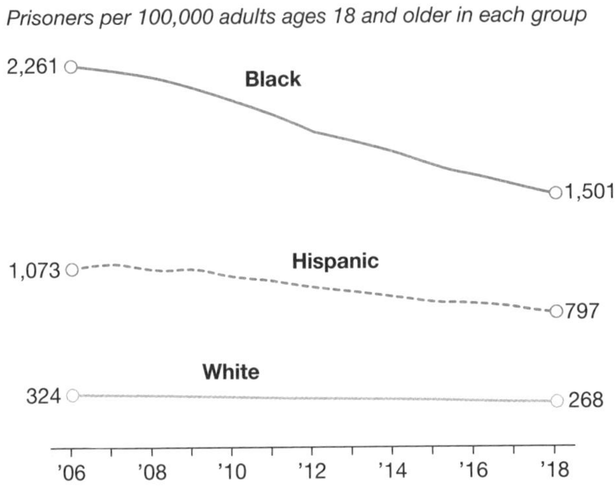

SOURCES: Bureau of Justice Statistics.

Pew Research Center (2016).

NOTE: Blacks and whites include those who report being only race and are non-Hispanic. Hispanics are of any race. Prisoners are those sentenced to more than a year in state or federal prison.

Importantly, teachers should try to remain neutral facilitators in classroom discourse. Most parents will welcome this guardrail articulated from the start. The job of social studies teachers is to build the skills of discourse and the understanding about the nature of government, civil society, and how all interact within the private sphere of our lives. While both of us are passionate about many contentious topics in our personal lives, as teachers we try to keep our opinions about open, political questions largely unknown to students because it is their job to formulate their own opinions without undue influence from the teacher.

Finally, once you have articulated the vision and the parameters of discourse, it is time to communicate this with the parent community. Does your school have a parent–teacher organization? If you worry that your parent community might react negatively to civil discourse, reach out to influential parents through small-group conversations. Practice many of the strategies outlined in the rest of this book, such as seeking understanding, establishing a sense of belonging, and practicing empathy when communicating with parents about the purpose of social studies instruction in your classroom, school, or district.

CLOSING REFLECTION

- What is the most compelling reason you read about why discomfort can no longer be avoided? Why does that resonate with you?
- How you would define the mission of your school to:
  - Your students?
  - Families of your students?
  - Community members?
  - Is it the same for all three? What role does having students engage in conversations about contentious topics play in meeting your mission?
- Why is it important that students be exposed to multiple perspectives in your classroom and school?
- How are the questions you use with students developed?
- Can you think of any compelling questions that you use with students that might need to be changed or adapted based on what you read?

Now that you have read this chapter, you should be able to complete the following:

- ✓ Find connections in your school or district mission or vision statements that support students engaging in civil discourse.
- ✓ In partnership with administrators, develop a vision statement for social studies education in your school or district that highlights the importance of civil discourse.
- ✓ Set parameters around which topics are open for discourse.
- ✓ Communicate the vision statement to parents and the larger community.

CHAPTER 2

Understanding

Gaining Clarity on the Meaning of Terms

Words have a magical power. They can either bring the greatest happiness or the deepest despair.

—Sigmund Freud

This chapter will help to prepare you to complete the following:

- ✓ Identify potentially contentious topics in your curriculum and standards.
- ✓ Reframe potentially contentious topics to make them less heated or intense.
- ✓ Sort potentially contentious topics by which discourse approach (dialogue, discussion, debate) is best suited to handle student conversations.
- ✓ Work with colleagues to develop a glossary of key terms and concepts related to civil discourse in your curriculum.

LANGUAGE SETS THE TONE

The words you choose are the "magical power" as noted by Sigmund Freud because they signal to students what is going to happen and what is expected of them. This chapter examines essential terms that truly impact the environment of your class. These terms are grouped together to provide guidance to ensure that you, your class, and your colleagues are all on the same page about the meaning of words that will be essential to students engaging in civil discourse. Do you and your students know the difference between dialogue and discussion or misinformation and disinformation? As you support student learning while engaging in discourse, the development of a shared understanding of the key terms in this chapter will be critical to success.

Take a moment and reflect on the following questions:

- Are there words that are used interchangeably with students that may not be interchangeable?
- What does it mean to be controversial instead of contentious?
- When having students engage in conversations, do you have clear goals in mind? How do you scaffold the different types of conversations to meet different goals?
- How do you help students process information that they hear inside and outside of the classroom to determine its reliability?

Words matter when it comes to helping us understand how we see ourselves and how other people see us based on the words that we choose when talking to them. Facing History and Ourselves (2021b, 2021c) has a lesson that focuses on the story of Niin and her experience as a kindergartener. She is an Anishinaabe woman of both Cree and Ojibway descent. Niin talked about the first time someone called her an Indian and the impact of the word:

> They [her classmates] were saying "Indian, Indian, Indian." And I was like what? I really didn't understand myself, first and foremost, as an "Indian." Right in the middle of when they were doing that, the bell rang and everybody just turned toward the door and started walking in. I remember looking down on the ground wondering, what are they talking about Indian, Indian, Indian? . . . I said, "Mom, what am I?" And she looked down at me and said really fast, "Were people asking you what you were?" I said, "Yes, they were calling me Indian." She said, "Tell them you're Canadian." . . . I think that's when I started learning that there were different kinds of people. (Facing History and Ourselves, 2021b)

Niin's classmates had an understanding of a word that they used to make fun of her. They wanted to hurt her and the word choice of "Indian" was able to deliver that message in a way that Niin's name could never do. The power of the word is reflected in Niin's mother telling her to tell her classmates that she was "Canadian." Although both Canadian and Indian were ways for Niin to define herself, based on societal discriminations and her classmates' understanding, Indian was the word that could impact Niin the most.

Have you ever been in a position where the words used impacted the entire conversation? As an educator, you are in a key position to make sure that the words used in your classroom are delivering the intended purpose and understanding. It might not always be as apparent as the teasing in Niin's story or the use of racial slurs, but this does not mean it is not impacting your students.

Sending a message through word choice is not new to First Nations people in the United States and Canada. The idea that Christopher Columbus "discovered" a continent of "savages" is a story that has been told in classrooms for decades (National Museum of the American Indian, 2018). Unfortunately, the use of words to harm others is not limited to First Nations people. In her essay "Orientation Day," Jennifer Wang (2001) talks about the confusion of the meaning behind a word: "During that time I also first heard the term 'chink,' and I wondered why people were calling me 'a narrow opening, usually in a wall.'" This is only part of her confusion growing up trying to understand what it means to be Chinese, American, or both.

Wang's experience related to derogatory terms is not unique to her, individuals of Asian descent, or even those of immigrant families and First Nations people. The power of words is understood by almost all who use them—even as young as kindergarteners, as told in Niin's story. In order to have students engage in the type of conversations necessary to build and support communities inside and outside of the classroom, an understanding of the words that are used is a must.

Each classroom, school building, and community has to be understood by the educators in order to give meaning to the words that frame the intent of what is trying to be communicated. Dr. Sally McConnell-Ginet (2020), author of *Words Matter: Meaning and Power*, tells us that "it is the socially structured practices and historically situated circumstances constituting our social lives that pour content into words, endowing them with meaning and power" (Blackwood, 2020). This is important to understand even down to a group as small as a classroom of students. McConnell-Ginet writes that each community has their own linguistic practices and "these communities can be small face-to-face ones like church choirs or book clubs, or they can be very large 'imagined' ones like nations."

OR OR *VERSUS*

It is also worth noting that we use the term *or* when talking about the word choices as opposed to *versus*. While the word *versus* in this context would be used to mean "as opposed to; in contrast to," the first definition according to Oxford Languages (2021b) is "against (especially in sports and legal use)." This may seem too nuanced; but if students are nudged even slightly into the idea that something like a sporting event or legal proceeding, then this will make a difference. Sporting events and legal proceedings have a winner and a loser or least that is the intent even in the case of a tie. The idea of having a winner or a loser can have implications in how students will approach this work (McAvoy & McAvoy, 2021), as the section on debate, discussion, or discourse will examine more in depth.

Oxford Languages (2021a) defines *or* as "used to link alternatives." If we step back from using *versus* and the idea of "against" and move toward *or* and the idea of "alternatives," this changes our classrooms. This change allows students to listen to different points of view not in terms of an absolute right answer with a "winner-take-all" champion, but rather as alternatives to one another without value or judgement being placed on them. For example, Joe's drive to the office has two choices that take almost the exact same amount of time (yes, he has timed them both multiple times). Are these two options in competition as a *versus* or are they alternatives to be separated by *or*?

The choice of the drive home, like many other decisions we make every day, is an alternative that we can choose depending on variables that may play a role. We do not usually say pizza *versus* burgers when deciding meals, nor should we push students to think that they have done something wrong if they are one side of a *versus*. The issues that our students will address in our classrooms need to come from the place of *or* as opposed to *versus*.

Each word choice that is made in the classroom may be small, but they all add up to set a tone. As you read through the following sections of four word groups, think about where they are currently used in your school or classroom. Decide what message you want to send to your students based on what is the goal of the learning that is taking place. The goal that you have in mind might be in conflict with your word choice, because words matter.

CONTENTIOUS OR CONTROVERSIAL

Are the words *contentious* and *controversial* synonyms when discussing topics to be addressed in your classroom? If you have been paying attention to word choice to this point in the book, you may have noticed a focus on the word *contentious* as opposed to *controversial*. This is intentional as part of subtle word choice cues to gently nudge how you approach what you are reading.

During the summer of 2020 following the murder of George Floyd, we found ourselves reading articles talking about the "controversy" surrounding the Black Lives Matter protests. When the Black Lives Matter movement was framed as "controversial," we struggled to accept the overarching idea that thinking that someone's life matters is a controversial stance. It was clear that the movement is a contentious subject for many, but is the core tenet of its motto inherently controversial or is it the how and why of the movement that is contentious?

When you hear the word *controversial*, what type of emotions does it elicit? Take a moment and reflect on the following questions to frame some of your thinking about this section.

- Do you believe that something that is "controversial" can be viewed as positive?
- Would you want there to be a "controversy" about something that you had done?

- Can people disagree about things and "agree to disagree"?
- Are there some topics that should never be discussed in a classroom regardless of context and student age?
- Who should have the final say in whether a topic is discussed in your classroom?
- What role do parents play in deciding what you teach?

We need to have a shared definition of the term *controversial* if we are going to determine which topics should be discussed in schools. A study by Byford et al. (2009) found that 72% of respondents believed that "students need to study controversial issues." But Ho et al. (2017) found that there was not a common definition for "controversial issues" and explored two potential interpretations.

The first interpretation centered on the idea of topics that some may deem to be inappropriate or objectionable. This idea was connected with the idea of "culture wars" as identified by Zimmerman (2005). The second interpretation explored the idea of topics that were "designed to help students investigate, evaluate, or deliberate issues that have multiple and competing views" (Ho et al., 2017). In this book, we clarify this by separating these two ideas into *controversial* for the former interpretation and *contentious* for the latter. The term *controversial* is often associated with a connotation that is negative, intense, or subject to extreme disapproval. The term *contentious* is associated with disagreement. We do not want students to see discourse topics as negatives, but rather as ideas that need more exploring in a way that is open to acceptance and understanding of those differences.

Something that is controversial will most likely be contentious, but is the opposite true? When a topic is labeled as contentious, does that mean that it has to be controversial? As sports fans, we both have seen plenty of contentious discussions that did not focus on what society would say is "controversial." Heated debates about the GOAT (Greatest of All Time) in different sports are a common occurrence among sports fans, as are discussions about whether "this certain team of one year would beat a different team of a different year," but few people would say these conversations qualify as controversial. Check out the results of a spring 2021 YouGov survey (Figure 2.1) and see if you agree with who is the GOAT and whether or not this list would be considered contentious or controversial (Bruce, 2021).

Looking at these words through a sports angle does not seem to have the two words as equals. Dictionary.com (2021) has a second definition of *controversial* to include "debatable," and this is what gave us pause in the summer of 2020. Is the idea that Black lives matter truly debatable? What does it mean for something to be debatable? Synonyms listed on Dictionary.com include "arguable" and "questionable," which seems to imply that if the idea that Black lives matter is controversial, then maybe the idea that Black lives matter is debatable. Do we want to have students debating whether or not a life "matters"?

If you dig a bit deeper, Merriam-Webster (2021c) lists an antonym of *controversial* as "safe." Importantly, Merriam-Webster (2021b) does *not* list the term safe as an antonym for *contentious*. Another antonym for safe is "dangerous," and we certainly want to avoid danger in our classrooms. Regardless of where educators stand on different contentious issues, we can probably all agree that our classrooms should be safe places where students learn to discuss and disagree respectfully on policy issues that are presented to them. Can we disagree in a peaceful manner even when the topic is contentious?

We also need to consider the meaning that students are bringing to the words we use in class. The topics that your students will most likely want to talk about are going to be ones that they are struggling with due to their contentious nature. Whether we are talking about the Second Amendment right to own a gun or the right of same-sex couples to marry, often

FIGURE 2.1 Results of a 2021 YouGov Survey on Who Americans Think Is the Greatest Athlete of All Time

Which athlete is the "greatest of all time" according to American sports fans?
American respondents who are fans of any sport were asked to choose who would be the "greatest of all time" in a series of head-to-head matchups. Figures shown are the % of times each athlete won their matchups.

		Athlete	Sport	Win percentage
1		**Muhammad Ali**	Boxing	78
2		**Michael Jordan**	Basketball	78
3		**Kareem Abdul-Jabbar**	Basketball	73
4		**Babe Ruth**	Baseball	73
5		**Jim Thorpe**	Pentathlon, decathlon, American football, baseball and basketball	72
6		**Jackie Robinson**	Baseball	70
7		**Jesse Owens**	Track and field	70
8		**Kobe Bryant**	Basketball	67
9		**Magic Johnson**	Basketball	66
10		**Michael Phelps**	Swimming	66

SOURCE: Bruce (2021).

times contentious issues strike at the core of how people define themselves.

It is important to separate people's identities from policy. People are not controversial. We do not want students thinking that someone's life or how they define themselves is controversial. This is why we as educators must be careful to make sure that we are not "debating" whether or not something is right or wrong; rather, we are focusing on how different people approach the policies related to these topics. This understanding is what will help keep students focused on the nuances of the topics instead of trying to pick a winner and loser among people's identities.

The key idea to take away is that using the word *contentious* as opposed to *controversial* may nudge your students in the direction of what you want them to do in your classroom and may help to ease the fears of parents who may be anxious about contentious topics. We encourage teachers to make the distinction explicit to both students and parents.

Action Step for Educators

Look through your curriculum and content standards to identify potentially contentious issues or topics. Consider making a list of potential controversial topics and reframing them as shown in Figure 2.2. Often a broadly framed topic can be more likely to cause intense emotion, while narrowing the scope can bring about a more nuanced conversation. The goal is to help students discuss ideas rather than exchange insults.

TYPES OF DISCOURSE: DIALOGUE, DISCUSSION, AND DEBATE

Once we set clear parameters around the type of topics we will discuss, it is time to gain clarity on the type of discourse

FIGURE 2.2 Examples of Reframing Contentious Topics

POTENTIALLY CONTROVERSIAL TOPICS	REFRAMING TO CONTENTIOUS ISSUES
Immigration	What should we do about unaccompanied minors at the border?
Gun control	How might we reduce the amount of gun-related violence in our communities?
Climate change	What is the role of the government in reducing air pollution in our town?

students will engage in. Too often, the terms *discussion* and *debate* are used interchangeably when they require different structures and result in different outcomes. What students believe they are about to do based on the term that is used plays a role in how they react to both the teacher and peers in the classroom.

When we are clear about the structure and goals, we increase the likelihood of student success. We believe there are three distinct types of discourse that should all be regular parts of social studies classes, but teachers must understand the particular uses of each of them. Figure 2.3 outlines each of the types of discourse, their purpose, student and teacher roles, and important considerations.

Dialogue

The spectrum for discourse starts on the "collaboration" end, with *dialogue* being the most informal and least structured conversation type. According to Wellman and Lipton (2017), "Dialogue promotes a spirit of inquiry within a group. The purpose is to generate multiple perspectives, encourage connection making between ideas and people, and develop shared

FIGURE 2.3 The Three Ds of Discourse: Dialogue, Debate, and Discussion

The 3Ds of Discourse

		DIALOGUE	DISCUSSION	DEBATE	
COLLABORATION	**Purpose**	Focused on building understanding of a topic; involves exploring it from many angles, active listening, and considering multiple points of view	Focused on idea exchange; participants may already have positions but are still open to hearing new information to shape their opinions on a topic	Focused on advancing a particular position, persuading, and refuting counter arguments; typically more formal with more advanced preparation	COMPETITION
	Student's Role	Openly explore the topic, including diverse research sources, actively listening, rephrasing, asking questions, and practicing empathy	Share what they are thinking, including research and reactions as to why one position may be the strongest	Requires advanced preparation usually on a particular outcome or position; actively responding to and refuting counter arguments against their position, and identifying holes in their logic, reasoning, or evidence of opposing positions	
	Teacher's Role	Model and explicitly teach active listening skills, empathy-building, finding common ground, and considering topics from multiple angles. Prompt students to consider the effects of the topic on multiple stakeholders	Encourage participation from all students, model and explicitly teach source analysis and reasoning skills, and prompt students to summarize each other's points and ask clarifying questions of each other's positions	Craft or guide students to craft the formal motion for debate, explicitly teaching argument and counter argument skills; often serves as the judge of who had the strongest argument based on neutral criteria such as sound logic and evidence	
	Things to Consider	Dialogue is best suited for topics where students are still learning about all of the angles and nuance is involved or for topics where emotions run high, so that there is a focus on the goal of understanding rather than identifying winning arguments and losing arguments	Discussion is best suited for conversations around policy topics where students have some background knowledge and opinions but also want to learn more and consider different ways to approach the topic	Debate is best suited for explicitly teaching persuasion skills and is best for topics where emotions do not run high and when students are assigned the sides randomly or take both positions rather than only sticking with their existing positions	

understandings. With dialogue there is no need to influence or agree" (p. 40). The goal of dialogue is a collaborative effort of information sharing to build a shared understanding. Kenneth Blanchard sets the perfect stage for a group dialogue by reminding us that "none of us is as smart as all of us" (Smith, 2011a). In a dialogue, conversation will flow as feels appropriate by the class, with participants working to bring new ideas to the table connected by a search for common ground and building off of the strengths of others.

Although minimal facilitation is usually necessary, educators should promote an atmosphere where "people freely and creatively explore issues, listen deeply to each other and suspend their own views in search of the truth" (Arnold, 2013). The building of a shared understanding occurs when there are clear expectations for students in regard to what type of feedback should be provided to others. "In dialogue, one submits one's best thinking, knowing that other peoples' reflections will help improve it rather than destroy it" (Metropolitan State University of Denver, 2008). The environment that allows for students to trust that others are there to support them is the focus of facilitation by the teacher. To achieve this classroom culture, teachers should focus on several key elements, including suspending judgement, listening to others with real concern, asking questions, exploring and reevaluating assumptions, and being willing to learn from new information to change thoughts and opinions (Hastwell, 2020; Metropolitan State University of Denver, 2008).

Discussion

Moving along the spectrum away from student collaboration and toward student competition, we find *discussion*. This is a term that is commonly used in classrooms when students are told that they are going to discuss or have a discussion about a certain topic or idea. In Figure 2.3, we have focused on the idea of a middle group between collaborative and competitive engagement by students. Using the definition of discussion from Wellman and Lipton (2017), the need for a middle group emerges as the goal of students shifts:

> Discussion breaks issues and problems into components and parts. The purpose is to generate and analyze ideas, clarify the distinctions between these ideas, and define success criteria. In discussion, group members critique and advocate, sort, and prioritize. (p. 40)

Therefore, discussion is more than a sharing of ideas and information like we see with dialogue, but is not fully competitive in terms of drawing up sides like in a debate.

Whereas dialogue is an opportunity to "enlarge ideas" (Arnold, 2013) and "find common ground" (Metropolitan State University of Denver, 2008), discussion is where "opposing views are presented and *defended* and the team searches for the best view to help make a team decision" (Arnold, 2013). Thus, discussion is semi-collaborative as participants are all on the same "side" and look to share information and ideas, yet "individual contributions often center around 'rightness' and are valued for it" (Metropolitan State University of Denver, 2008) as the group seeks consensus on a "best" answer.

In dialogue, it is key for participants to "suspend their own views" (Arnold, 2013) and for educators to work to facilitate the conversation as such. Since an important part of a discussion is "choosing sides" (Garmston & Wellman, quoted in Brown Easton, 2015) in order to decide a best answer, listening is more focused on being "able to insert one's own perspective" (Metropolitan State University of Denver, 2008) and defend that perspective. Therefore, the role of teacher facilitation moves from ensuring that all voices are heard without judgement to one of making sure that there is an understanding of what the positions are. Walter Parker (2010) tells us, "When a group seeks understanding together, it works to create, plumb, and clarify meanings and explanations. When it forges a decision, it weighs alternatives and tries to decide among them" (p. 2826). What starts as a collaborative process moves toward a competitive process, and support is crucial in helping students understand what the intended goal is and that each step along the way will be facilitated with clear processes.

Debate

On the furthest end of the competitive spectrum lies *debate*. This is another word that is commonly used in classrooms, although maybe not always in the proper context. Using the term *debate* out of context may cause issues to arise in the classroom when students bring their own understanding of the word to the conversation. According to Garmston and Wellman,

> Debate is an extreme form of discussion, in which the format dictates that people take sides and advocate for that side, rebutting points from the other side. Debates are usually structured and formal; they leave no room for compromise or building on others' ideas. (Quoted in Brown Easton, 2015)

Whether intentionally or not, if students in their mind believe that the conversation is one that leaves no room for compromise, then this limits the flexibility of the potential interactions between the students.

The idea of what a student may think about a conversation when it is framed as a debate is evident in the sample sentences provided by Merriam-Webster (2021d):

- "Our polite chat about politics became a *heated* debate."
- "The case sparked a *raging* public debate on property rights."
- "The subject was *hotly* debated."

The words associated with debate (heated, raging, and hotly) are all of the things that educators worry about in the back of their mind when they think about contentious topics. The thought of *what happens if*... usually focuses on the topic getting too "heated" and before you know it the "raging" has gotten out of control and potentially the events of your class become a "hotly" discussed topic of administrators and the community. With all of this in mind, we are by no means suggesting that students should not debate, but we do want to be clear about when debates should occur, what topics should be debated, and how they should be structured. The purpose of this section is to help remind teachers about the power of words and the potential ideas that students already have about them.

We believe that debate is best suited for teaching students the skills of persuasion and argumentation, often around topics that are not emotionally charged. The higher the emotional charge, the further away from competition we should go. Here are some examples we like to use as debate topics with students:

- Should the voting age be lowered?
- Should we end daylight savings time?
- Should the school week be four days instead of five?

When the conversation is framed as a debate, the emotional shift immediately begins. In a 2021 interview, Carlee Goldberg, Triangle Debate League President at Duke University, said:

> Telling students we're having a debate versus a discussion dictates the outcome. It's the difference between students entering a classroom with an us-against-them mentality or ready for a conversation with limitless options and results. Both debates and discussions are extraordinarily important in civic education and in building lifelong civic skills. But they teach fundamentally different

> things. Debate teaches you how to persuade, discussion teaches you how to evaluate and understand. Students need both to navigate contentious issues and come out with solutions and not a standstill.

Students entering into a debate have a goal of winning. We see this after every presidential debate; within minutes of the conclusion, there are "instant polls" that determine the winner. The next day, there are a multitude of articles about "winners and losers from last night's debate." When students are told that they will debate about a topic, the shift in mindset moves away from any sort of collaborative effort with those on the other side. Students know that "the goal of debate is to defeat the other's position" and they check in along the way by asking themselves, "Am I winning this argument?" (Indian Prairie School District 204, n.d.).

In a classroom debate it is important for the facilitating educator to be aware of a couple of major dynamic shifts away from dialogue and even discussion. First and foremost, there should be some process for determining how each side is doing and possibly a way to determine which side wins in the end. This might be as simple as "polling" a group of neutral observers, such as other students (similar to a presidential debate), or as complicated as a scoring system (more similar to a boxing match). Either way, when debating, students will look to some sort of answer about how they have done in determining which side won.

It is also key to facilitate the debate with an understanding that it is different from a discussion in terms of cooperation. While a discussion also gives a path to determine the best answer, it is achieved by working together and building off of others' ideas. In a classroom debate, opposing ideas are countered and opposed as a way to defeat or discredit the opposing side. Students on the same side of the debate will inevitably work together because they are unified in competition against the other side. Listening to learn is replaced by listening to refute.

Debates also lose the flexibility of ideas and thoughts as the purpose of listening changes. When debating the idea of listening to another person to find strengths across common ground is replaced by listening to find weakness in order to elevate one's own ideas. During a discussion, the goal is to put a wide variety of ideas on the table before deciding—this often means that students may promote multiple points of view about what is best. Due to the structure of a debate, changing positions is rare, as the goal is to show your side has the best answer.

We strongly encourage you to understand the difference between the 3Ds in this chapter (dialogue, discussion, and debate) and to incorporate them in your classrooms. Each of these types of communication has its own unique set of skills that must be highlighted and practiced by students in order for them to be successful. As the educator charged with facilitating these conversations, make sure to understand the differences with the 3Ds and develop classroom structures that support student success.

Students will be successful when they know what type of conversation is happening and what the intended outcome is. The way we communicate with each other is determined by the situation, purpose, and goal of each interaction. In order for our students to be successful in our communities both inside and outside of our schools, we must equip them with the ability to participate in all of these settings.

Action Step for Educators

Consider sorting the list of potentially contentious topics you created in the previous section into the type of discourse best suited for that topic. Figure 2.4 provides an example.

FIGURE 2.4 Example of Topics and Types of Discourse

DIALOGUE	DISCUSSION	DEBATE
• Immigration • Gun control • Equity in college admissions	• Inheritance tax • Single-use plastic tax • Vaccine mandates	• Minimum wage • Voting age • Days of the school week

Different communities find different topics to be more emotionally charged than others, so we encourage you to consider your students, parents, and larger community as you are making the list.

MISINFORMATION, DISINFORMATION, AND FAKE NEWS

The struggles of working to make sure that we are well versed in the "truth" is not a new one. Mark Twain famously said, "A lie can travel halfway around the world while the truth is putting on its shoes." With this quote, the American author showed that he understood not only the world in which he lived but also the world beyond his lifetime. But was Mark Twain as prophetic as we make him out to be? Or are we thinking of the wisdom of Winston Churchill?

We have heard this quote attributed to both Mark Twain and Winston Churchill, but it only takes the simplest of Google searches to see the trouble with this accepted "fact." There is no evidence to show that either Mark Twain or Winston Churchill ever said it. The Quote Investigator (2014) does a great job of showing how this quote evolved over time from Jonathan Swift's original version, "Falsehood flies, and the truth comes limping after it," in 1710. The inconvenient truth about who spoke about truth is so ingrained in American pop culture that the *New York Times* used this "Mark Twain" quote as the headline example when they examined how quotes get misattributed (Chokshi, 2017).

As educators, how are we supposed to know what is the truth when even quotes about the truth are not truthful? At the most basic level, both students and teachers need to be able to know when we are talking about facts and when our individual perspective is pushing what we want to believe. In her book, *The Trouble With Reality,* author Brooke Gladstone (2017) says,

> Part of the problem stems from the fact that facts, even a lot of facts, do not constitute reality. Reality is what forms after we filter, arrange, and prioritize those facts and marinate them in our values and traditions. Reality is personal. (p. 2)

We are not ready to accept the idea of "alternative facts," but we must be ready to confront the reality that each person we interact with brings a unique perspective to each conversation.

The "values and traditions" that Gladstone refers to will drive students and adults to look for information that matches their perspectives. We actively search for information that confirms our beliefs while ignoring information that challenges our beliefs. This includes ignoring strong evidence that goes against what we believe to be true (Journell, 2021a). With this in mind, we will not be able to just tell students to do a better job of fact checking or researching. This does not work with adults, nor will it work with our students.

According to a 2016 Pew Research Center survey, 14% of Americans "shared a political news story online they knew at the time was made up" (Barthel et al., 2020). With so much attention on "fake news" in recent years, the number has gotten somewhat better, but a 2019 Statista survey showed that

10% of Americans had shared news or information online that they "knew at the time was made up" (Watson, 2020). These same surveys showed a drastic increase in the people who had unknowingly shared information that they later found out was made up, with a jump from 16% in 2016 to 49% in 2019 (see Figure 2.5).

Of course, students also bring heavily biased information into the classroom (Segall et al., 2019). This means that teachers, while remaining relatively neutral about contentious topics, do have the responsibility to address poor information or prejudices that students bring to classroom discourse (Journell, 2021b). This challenge must be faced head on by acknowledging that we all have different perspectives and then building a framework of understanding what types of information we have at our disposal.

To understand the issue of wrestling with the inundation of information that our students are exposed to every day (Kwan, 2019), we should start with common definitions for

FIGURE 2.5 Sharing of Misinformation Online in 2016 and 2019

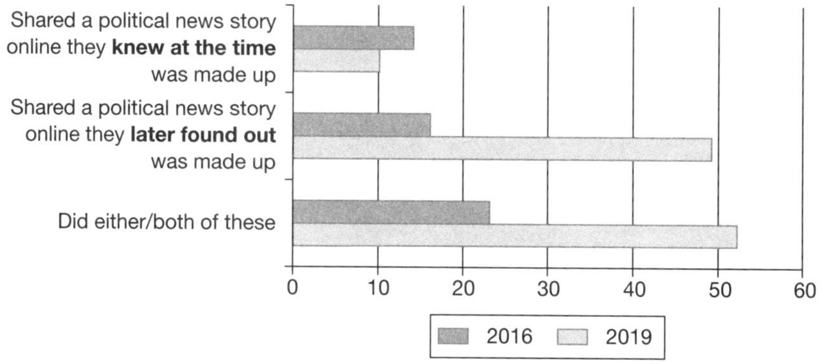

SOURCES: Survey conducted Dec. 1–4, 2016. "Many Americans Believe Fake News Is Sowing Confusion." Pew Research Center.

Pew Research Center data from Barthel et al. (2020), and Statista data from Watson (2020), respectively.

staff and students. As much as society currently looks to Facebook as one of the leading causes of spreading incorrect information, they understand the importance of defining the problem at hand. In 2017, Facebook reported the following:

> The term "fake news" has emerged as a catch-all phrase to refer to everything from new articles that are factually incorrect to opinion pieces, parodies and sarcasm, hoaxes, rumors, memes, online abuse, and factual misstatements by public figures that are reported in otherwise accurate news pieces. The overuse and misuse of the term "fake news" can be problematic because, without common definitions, we cannot understand or fully address these issues. (Weedon et al., 2017, p. 4)

What does Facebook mean when they talk about the "misuse" of the term *fake news*?

In the book, *Unpacking Fake News: An Educator's Guide to Navigating the Media With Students* edited by Dr. Wayne Journell, Dr. H. James Garrett (2019) lays out three distinct types of fake news based on the intent of who created it and the intent of anyone sharing it: tabloid untruths, targeted disinformation and misinformation, and weaponized phrases. See Figure 2.6 for an explanation of each.

Tabloid untruths are the first of these and the most straightforward—they are most famously known as the original "fake news." Entertainment is the goal of this type of news and it ranges from completely unbelievable to social commentary. Tabloids produce stories about alien abductions, *The Onion* gives us satire and parody, and *The Daily Show*, though researched for accuracy, makes light of issues as a way to drive home a usually politically biased point. Even though there is a spectrum of how much fact is contained in

FIGURE 2.6 Types of Fake News

WHAT TYPE OF FAKE NEWS IS IT?				
	TABLOID UNTRUTHS	TARGETED DISINFORMATION	TARGETED MISINFORMATION	WEAPONIZED PHRASES
Purpose	Entertainment to expand profits	Information that is shared to harm others and have them focus on a point of view	Amplified disinformation that is shared to focus on a point of view	Determining the validity of the information shared
Level of accuracy	Ranges depending on the story	Created with inaccurate information	True to the sharer but not accurate information	Dependent on the sharers' knowledge of content

these different examples, creators of this content purposefully seek to entertain and hope that others share their stories to widen the audience of people who are entertained in order to expand profits.

Things get a lot more complicated when looking at disinformation and misinformation. This type of fake news is "a plausible, though fabricated, story that is disseminated through social media using sophisticated targeting strategies" (Garrett, 2019). While the intent of fake news in a "tabloids untruth" sense is to entertain, disinformation is "false content that is intentionally disseminated with intent to harm" (Wardle, 2019, p. 8). The creators of disinformation know that what they are creating is not accurate, but any pretense of entertainment is secondary to the attempt to influence the consumers of the information to believe a certain point of view.

According to Merriam-Webster (2021e), *disinformation* is created "in order to influence public opinion or obscure the truth." This is achieved when those other than the creators share the information. This is mostly done by those who are not aware that the information is inaccurate. When we unintentionally share information that is inaccurate, we amplify its reach. This is when the content becomes *misinformation* as defined by Wardle (2019). Again, not everyone who shares disinformation does it unknowingly.

The last idea of fake news that your students will have to come to understand is the use of "fake news" as a *weaponized phrase*. The issue at hand is not access to information, but rather whether we can sort through and process the information that is available to us. The amount of information at our fingertips can be used to make us either smarter or more ignorant, depending on how we use it (Wineburg et al., 2016). This is the environment where using the term *fake news* to discredit news and information as you see fit has been allowed to flourish. When the term *fake news* carries so much potential to disrupt how our students see the world, we must take measures to make sure that proper use of the terminology is emphasized to truly deweaponize the term. Claire Wardle (2019) at First Draft has created a spectrum (Figure 2.7) that shows the seven types of mis- and disinformation and how they relate to each other. If we are going to *de*weaponize the phrase, then we must all know what we are actually talking about instead of throwing around the term *fake news*.

As noted in Chapter 1, we must get our students involved in the world around them, but as Chapter 2 has shown us, we must be careful with the language we use with our students as we encourage these conversations. The speed and pace of change as well as the rapid spread of ideas—including those that are factually incorrect—change the dynamics of civic engagement today and challenge the very nature of democracy (Weedon et al., 2017). These challenges are ones in which schools and educators have a huge role to play.

FIGURE 2.7 Seven Types of Mis- and Disinformation

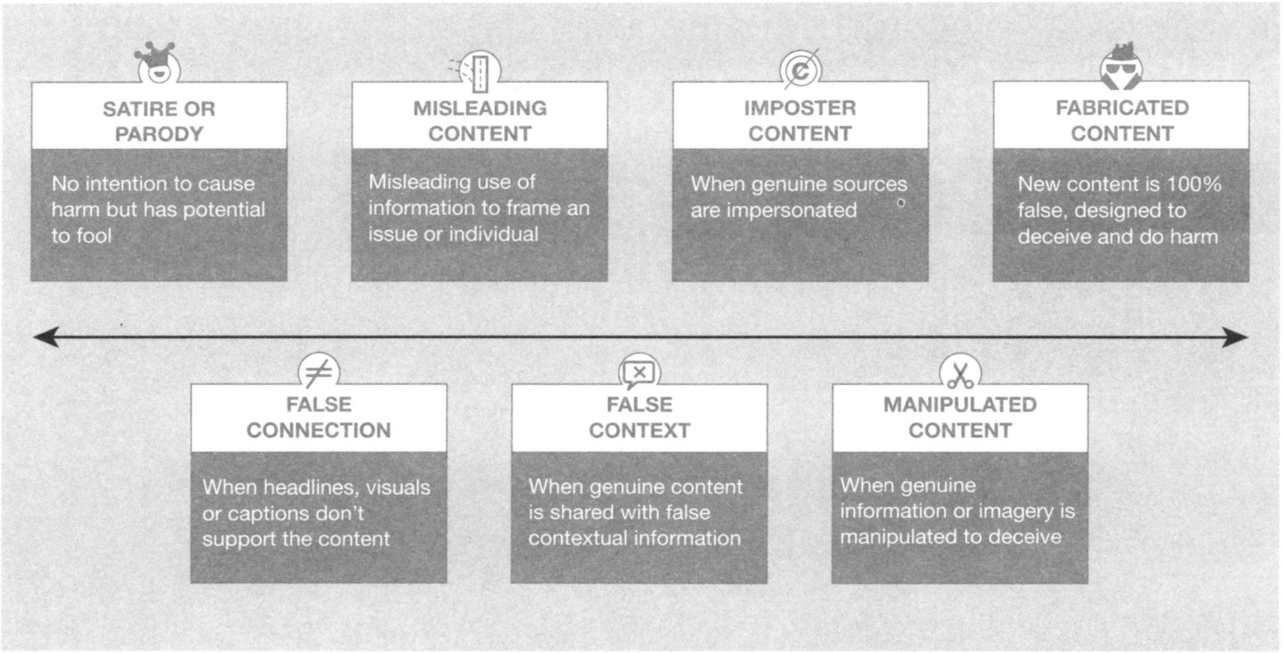

SOURCE: Wardle (2019), reprinted with permission from *First Draft*.

Even as schools pick up the mantle to do this important work, it does not mean that it will be easy work.

> In this time of widespread dissemination of alternative facts and misinformation, teachers have a responsibility to turn classrooms into spaces where reason and inquiry trump ignorance and hyperbole. But doing so often requires teachers to take a stance regarding what issues are worthy of deliberation and what information warrants consideration, and the decisions teachers make may be risky, as teachers are generally expected to be politically neutral, and expressions of their political beliefs can expose them to accusations of bias. (Journell, 2016)

The rest of this book is intended to show educators and districts how we all—educators, administrators, families, and community members included—can play a role in developing classrooms where this difficult but important work can be safely and properly done.

Action Step for Educators

Now that we've considered several terms and clarified their uses and meaning, consider collaborating with other social studies teachers and leaders in your school or district to make a glossary of key terms and concepts related to civil discourse. This will greatly help you to communicate the purpose and ensure everyone is on the same page about the words we use to foster discourse in our classrooms. Once created, post it on your class webpage, include it in a school newsletter, or share it with parents at back-to-school night or parent–teacher conferences.

CLOSING REFLECTION

- What words are you going to focus on making sure that all students and educators share an understanding of? How will you make sure that a shared understanding occurs?
- How do you anticipate using a progression of dialogue, discussion, and debate to meet the different goals of your classroom?
- Why is it important for both you and your students to be able to discuss the different types of sources of information that are available? What barriers do you anticipate in having these discussions?
- As this book moves into laying out a framework for planning activities in your classroom, what are you most hoping to learn?

Now that you have read this chapter, you should be able to complete the following:

✓ Identify potentially contentious topics in your curriculum and standards.

✓ Reframe potentially contentious topics to make them less heated or intense.

✓ Sort potentially contentious topics by which discourse approach (dialogue, discussion, debate) is best suited to handle student conversations.

✓ Work with colleagues to develop a glossary of key terms and concepts related to civil discourse in your curriculum.

CHAPTER 3

Belonging

Establishing a Classroom Community

I never teach my pupils, I only attempt *to provide the conditions in which they can learn.*

—Albert Einstein

This chapter will help to prepare you to complete the following:

- ✓ Develop protocols for how to handle inappropriate comments and untimely questions in your classroom in order to know how you will react when the unexpected happens.
- ✓ In accordance with school and district policies, create a list of non-negotiable student agreements for your classroom.
- ✓ Identify places in your classroom where student voice and input can be included in the development of classroom agreements.

(Continued)

(Continued)

- ✓ Explore ways to get to know your students and their home lives as well as the values and traditions of the school and community.
- ✓ Collect examples of classroom agreements for students to examine when developing their own.
- ✓ Create a plan for how classroom agreements will be posted, reinforced, and communicated with administrators and parents.

Teachers are always looking for the next great lesson plan idea or resource for their classrooms. Almost anything can spark an idea for a teacher that they hope will grab the interest of their students and lead to learning engagement. In our drive for the "perfect" lesson plan that will inspire our students, it can become easy to forget that building the foundation of our classroom needs to include building a classroom culture for and with our students. That classroom culture starts before they even step foot into our classroom.

Take a moment and reflect on the following questions:

- How do you plan for both the expected and unexpected in your classroom?
- What do you do so that your students (and families) feel a sense of belonging in your classroom?
- What role do students play in the development of your classroom rules and agreements?
- How do you ensure that your classroom contract "lives" throughout the year?

DAY ZERO: PLANNING FOR PROTOCOLS, POLICIES, AND PROCEDURES

Planning for having conversations about contentious topics in your classroom begins before students enter your classroom. We have already addressed how word choice can make a difference with you and your students. Understanding these words, knowing how you will use them, and getting the necessary people on the same page (grade-level team, department, building, etc.) is part of the preplanning for the school year.

In addition to shared terminology, day-zero planning should include developing your protocols, policies, and procedures (3Ps) that you will share with your students on day one and beyond. These can be developed at the individual classroom, grade or department, or school level, but each teacher needs to have some ownership of the 3Ps and feel comfortable with them in order to use them successfully. The 3Ps help provide expectations and guidance for your students to keep the classroom a safe space, and they will be your "safety net" to refer back to when things go differently than expected.

Let's start with protocols. A protocol is a plan that specifies what to do in defined situations. Examples of protocols include how attendance is taken, how homework is submitted, and what students are to do during a fire drill. We will talk about classroom rules and planning for what student conversations will look like later on; for now, think about all of the things that you know will happen at some point and develop protocols for them.

Just as important in planning for the expected is planning for the unexpected. This is why we have fire drills. With the protocols in place for what happens in case of a fire, we are able to practice them. Practice prepares for the "unexpected" because there is a set of expectations that will be followed to get everyone out of the building safely. Any drills that you and your students do during the year are examples of protocols to protect against the unexpected.

What are the types of "unexpected" events that you should be thinking about during your day-zero planning?

- How are you going to handle the "unrelated" question about a contentious topic that is asked at an inopportune time?
- What will be your first reaction to a student who makes an inappropriate comment?
- What happens when a student shares sensitive information about themselves or someone else that should not have been shared?
- What happens when a student asks about a topic that you (the teacher) aren't familiar with or well versed in?
- How will you react when students start arguing among themselves before you are aware that a conversation on a contentious topic is happening?
- What will you do when an "outsider" (another teacher, parent, or class guest) says something that contradicts something that you have said?

You do not know when or under what circumstances any of the above will happen, but recognizing that they might happen allows you to develop your protocols to handle the situation. Usually when there is an issue with how a teacher reacts to a student, it is because the teacher reacted in the moment without having thought about the situation ahead of time.

Provide yourself a safe space to handle the unexpected by knowing what you will say to your student(s) in a situation like the examples provided. This might mean letting the student know that you can talk more after class. Perhaps you have time built into your schedule to allow for any thoughts or ideas from the day to be discussed. Practicing a scripted response to an inappropriate comment helps to manage your emotions in that particular moment. For a lot of these situations, there is not a perfect response, but there are a lot of responses that only add to the emotions and escalate a tough situation. Scan the QR code for potential situations with ideas and resources for how to handle them.

> Scan the QR code for ideas and resources on how to handle unexpected conversations and situations in your classroom.

After creating protocols, think about what policies of yours are non-negotiable. Policies are the classroom rules and agreements that govern how the class runs and how students interact on a day-to-day basis. This chapter will address how to work on developing classroom agreements beyond the foundation you provide for them. Here are some things to consider when developing your non-negotiable classroom policies:

- Are there any school or district rules that must be followed in every classroom?
    - For example, certain websites are off limits.
- What type of agreements have worked well in the past and which ones are you comfortable with?
    - For example, students are allowed to listen to their headphones during certain parts of your classroom and this has worked well for you in the past.
- What type of agreements have not worked in the past and which ones are you uncomfortable with?
    - For example, students cannot bring food or drink into your classroom, as this might be up to teacher discretion but you have had issues with it in the past.

Later in this chapter we will talk more about creating classroom contracts based on agreements developed by your students, but day-zero planning is an opportunity to decide which policies must be incorporated into the classroom contract.

Procedures are the last of your 3Ps that you can begin planning for during day zero. A procedure is a set of instructions that describes how students will engage in civil discourse around a specific topic or question. These procedures are how your students will work as individuals and as a group to participate in the learning in your classroom. Many of the ideas that will be covered in Chapters 4 and 5 are grounded in developing procedures that students practice until they are second nature.

Students, like all human beings, struggle to process both procedural and emotional information at the same time. Therefore, we encourage you to be transparent about what you expect your students to do during classroom discourse and practice until they are able to transfer their processing power to handle the information and emotions related to contentious topics. Day-zero planning means knowing the pedagogical moves and strategies that you will practice and reinforce with your students as they move from day one of class all the way up to the most contentious topics.

DAY ONE: CLASSROOM COMMUNITY

Relationships can be hard. Often, the people we love the most are the people who can also cause us the most frustration and pain. But relationships are still indispensable to human development (Laursen & Collins, 2009; St. Petersburg—USA Orphanage Research Team, 2008). Humans need each other. Knowing that disagreement is inevitable can help us to lay the foundation for civil discourse. And establishing a culture of belonging is the cornerstone of fostering respectful conversations about contentious topics.

Nichelle recalls walking into a diverse classroom and seeing the phrase "We are familia" with images of over 75 students from all backgrounds and experiences surrounding the vibrant phrase. She was so excited to see this phrase because it set a tone. She was intrigued to see what "We are familia" actually looks like in this classroom. With further observation, she learned that *familia* meant family in both Swahili and Spanish. It reminded her that the concept of family—though different and obscure depending on experience—meant something no matter where we came from. This bond is the tie that held this class together.

We can build classroom culture by comparing it to the concept of family or community. How do we as educators ensure that our community is functional and ready to have the conversations needed to resolve disagreements, determine critical decisions, grow together, and heal when we inevitably disappoint each other? How do we exhibit a functional community at school?

Step one is to ensure that the teacher and students build a shared understanding of how they want to operate as a class community. What is a community? What constitutes a community? What happens when a community gets along? What happens when a community does not agree? All these questions should be defined and modeled in the classroom, starting on day one.

A family is defined as a socially recognized group that forms an emotional connection in a society. An emotional connection alludes to the fact that emotions will always be a part of the family, and even when we feel hurt, upset, disappointed, and angry with each other, this does not change the fact that we are still part of a family. The classroom is a wonderful place to model the idea that no matter what, we are all in this together! Being together requires that all members feel included, understood, heard, and accepted.

From the beginning it is important to remind students that no matter how close a family or community may be, families and communities do disagree and even fight from time to time. The strength of a classroom is one that allows for disagreements among members, but does not break the bonds that have been developed. During conversations in our classrooms, the goal is not for everyone to reach the same conclusion, but rather for everyone to feel that their point of view has been heard and understood by others.

Strong communities thrive on the concepts of belonging and worthiness. These human experience concepts are important in our larger communities as well as to the families we establish in our classrooms. Everyone must feel and understand that they belong and are worthy of being heard and seen. It is important to establish the environment for students to understand that we as educators will do this.

Part of establishing the environment to be understood is knowing that not everyone will agree with you. Preparing for contentious conversations starts with laying the groundwork that while we may disagree, we strive to not be disagreeable. Ask students how they believe people should talk with each other when they disagree. Discuss experiences that they have had with others where they felt okay after someone disagreed with them and compare to times where they feel that the disagreement did not go well. These conversations will help set the stage for developing a classroom contract.

Helping students understand the different ways that we talk and listen to each other is crucial in having conversations in the classroom and goes beyond a classroom contract. Joe would have a discussion at the beginning of the school year with each of his classes about the differences between teasing and bullying. He had seen enough classroom conversations start to break down under the guise of "Mr. Schmidt, I was just teasing" to know that this had to be directly addressed from the beginning by talking about the differences between "just teasing" and when it was more than that.

To help keep these differences at the forefront for his students, Joe had an anchor chart of the work of Dr. Barbara Coloroso (2010) listing the characteristics of both teasing and bullying. Any time comments between students seemed to be more about personal attacks rather than the topic at hand, this anchor chart was referenced to determine if it really was "just teasing" as the offending student would often say. Making this an important part of the classroom culture would lead to students calling out the chart about comments that they felt crossed the line, and Joe was more of an arbitrator as the classroom began to govern itself like a healthy community does when disputes occur.

As educators it is our ultimate responsibility to build a community of trust and transparency in our classrooms, and we must remember that it is our job to set the tone to be able to say, "We are a family or community." So how do we establish the concept of belonging and worthiness?

1. **Learn and call students by their name.** The very first step is for teachers and students to learn each other's names as soon as possible. Most teachers do a great job at this, but at times students are not sure who is sitting next to them on a daily basis. A person's name is the first identifier they are given. In many cultures a name carries a story of identity and pride. Utilizing a student's name from day one says, "I see you and acknowledge that you are a part of our community." Make sure if you choose to call students by last name that you do so for all and vice versa. Taking a few minutes each day to greet each other by name, practice saying each other's names, and learn something about each other is an investment in time that will pay off handsomely once we start discussing contentious topics.

2. **When students enter the school, let's welcome them with a smile.** Smiles should come from the principal, the secretary, the teachers—all school staff. This smile doesn't have to be exaggerated but students should feel as though you want to be there no matter what is going on in your life. When students arrive at your classroom, greet them. As students enter the classroom, teachers should have established what Nichelle likes to call the "daily grand gesture." The grand gesture establishes that students have entered their safe place. This safe place is reliable and consistent. It is a grand gesture because this is your first attempt to show students who you are and what to expect.

   Students should expect this grand gesture daily, and it should set the tone for all of the learning and investigating that will occur in your class. They should know whenever they approach or enter your room, this will occur. The grand gesture can be as big as a synchronized dance move to just a simple "Good morning" or "Good afternoon." Through social media, we have seen an increasing number of ways teachers welcome students to the class. Teachers have started differentiating this experience depending on the child by providing a small choice board for students at the door where they can choose how they want to greet the teacher. Remember, whatever you decide, it should be comfortable for both you and the students; this will ensure that it is done daily because you will all be looking forward to it.

3. **Discuss what it means to be a community.** Students come to school with their own personal definition of what a community is. This definition is defined by experiences and events they have seen in their lives. You want to ensure that as a class or school you agree upon your definition of what community is. To do this, the first thing you must do is establish what a community is and is not. Show examples of a community and nonexamples

of a community. After you establish a definition of community, then discuss what communities do:

- Communities agree.
- Communities disagree.
- Communities have similar opinions and interests.
- Communities have different opinions and interests.

Allow students to then state in their own words what is a community and how they treat one another. At the end of this activity you want students to be articulate that a community works together and looks out for one another. Communities disagree but it does not change that they still care about each other and work together to protect each other.

CLASS AGREEMENTS, CONTRACTS, AND AFFIRMATIONS

Class Agreements

In addition to teacher non-negotiables, we can co-create class agreements. These can be developed from your school's core values statement. Consider this example from a middle school:

As students at Excellence Middle School, we will exude our core values of PRIDE: perseverance, respect, integrity, diversity, and empathy.

- We will have PRIDE in the halls of Excellence Middle School.
  - Persevere when learning gets difficult.
  - Respect each Excellence community member with
  - Integrity, believing the best in each member by embracing the
  - Diversity of the community we belong to.
  - Exude excellence by being Empathetic to community members.

Using these core values, students can co-construct agreements such as these:

- We agree to work hard and not give up. (Perseverance)
- We agree to respect each other. (Respect)
- We agree to be honest and open in class. (Integrity)
- We agree to embrace our differences. (Diversity)
- We agree to listen and understand everyone's perspective. (Empathy)

Class agreements like this one allow the class to have established norms that are aligned to the campus core values or mission statements.

Contracts

Every community has an agreed-upon set of rules or laws. The rules or laws are established so that the members of the community can work and live collaboratively. To be collaborative, we must have a clear understanding of expectations. The best way to have clear expectations is to formulate those expectations collaboratively. We must remember that this is a living document and do our best to ensure that everyone has participated in this process.

In Nichelle's first "real year" of teaching, she taught eleventh-grade students. She calls this year the "the real year" because it challenged everything she learned in her previous first-grade classroom. While she had all of the classroom rules up at the beginning of the year, she realized that by the beginning of the second semester she needed to do something else. She had read *First Days of School* (Wong & Wong, 1997) and decided to start the semester with a classroom contract.

Through images and videos Nichelle established what chaos could look like without structure. At the time, she was teaching United States history. She decided to help students acquire the concept of a classroom contract by utilizing examples from history and pop culture, such as the Mayflower Compact, the House of Burgesses, scenes from *Lord of the Flies*, and a very short clip from *Big Brother*. These sources helped to establish what a contract can and has looked like. Then as a class they defined what a classroom contract was and what it was not. They came to a common definition that the classroom contract was to be an agreement between the students and teacher on how the class will be structured so that everyone felt respected and had a voice. By the end of that first day, they had a big picture of what a classroom contract was and all were in agreement.

By the end of day two, the students and teacher had five big pieces of butcher paper sheets hanging from the cinder block walls, showing the classroom contract of each class period. Each sheet highlighted respect for others. This was very different from the rules Nichelle had placed on the walls earlier that year. Nichelle began to use the classroom contract to guide expectations of how the class would function on a daily basis. Over time, the process became more structured and streamlined where she was able to receive the most efficient results and commitment from the students. By year three, students began to collaborate across class periods and it became one classroom contract. This story shares the importance of involving students and taking the time to invest in building these agreements.

Here are some tips on how to establish a classroom contract in your class.

1. Find examples of social contracts.
    a. Some examples used previously include the Mayflower Compact and the Virginia House of Burgesses.
2. Students should brainstorm things that they fear could go wrong in this class or previous classes. Encourage students to think of possible fears they may have or had

when teachers talked about topics they did not like. How did that make them feel? What do you wish the teacher would have done? What do you wish other students would have done?

   a. Try to provide an example.
   b. Provide sentence starters to help in this process for younger students.

3. The teacher shares the list of non-negotiable agreements for the class. Students use this list as the foundation and continue to build their own agreements as a class. Most non-negotiables are rules that tend to be campus rules and expectations.
   a. We will respect everyone.
   b. Name-calling or taunting classmates will not be permitted.
   c. There is no bullying of classmates.
4. Then students go to assigned groups and look over the list that they had individually composed. In the groups, students share their ideas as well as collaborate on solutions to those ideas. We encourage the use of large chart paper for students to map out their thinking.
5. Students share the collective results from their respective groups.
6. The teacher creates a ballot/poll for students to vote individually or via groups depending on the culture.
   a. Individually: send the percentages or show the tally of votes.
   b. Group: allow students to decide what to keep or get rid of.
7. Turn the ideas into rules that are student friendly.
8. Have students sign individually. Hold a signing ceremony and make it a monumental event. Invite your

administrator to visit your class during the process. Send personal handwritten or virtual invites for classroom contract signing day.

9. Reference and edit the contract if needed. Your classroom contract should be a living document. Discuss edits or revisions as needed.

Centering Your Classroom Contract

Creating and signing the classroom contract is only the beginning of bringing it to life in your classroom. Classroom contracts and classroom rules are only as effective as what happens with them in the days and weeks after they are written and signed. It is the role of the classroom teacher and district administration to help ensure that the practices, protocols, and procedures spelled out by the classroom contract live beyond the day they were written.

In order to hold students accountable to what was agreed upon, educators must hold themselves accountable to both modeling what is expected and working to ensure that the classroom contract is not a "one-and-done" activity. To ensure that you are able to clearly and consistently model what is expected of students, we encourage you to start by focusing on the non-negotiables and modeling what is expected by discussing what this "looks like" and what this "does not look like" in your classroom. By starting with the non-negotiables, you set the stage for how these support the additional ideas that the students brought to the contract.

After you model what the non-negotiables look like and do not look like, have students add examples of both categories for each agreement in the classroom contract until all parts of the classroom contract have been discussed. Make sure that there is room in the conversations to discuss what happens when the agreements are not followed. Do the students have a way to signal that they feel as though their classroom contract has been broken? How will a breach of contract be remedied, and what is the role of both the educator and students in handling this process?

While there are countless ways in which a breach of the classroom contract can be handled, students should be involved in determining what that process will look like—just like the creation of the contract. The most important part is making sure that students know *what* will happen, *when* it will happen, and *who* will participate in correcting any issues with the classroom contract.

Once the classroom contract is in place and expectations are set for "living" this document on an ongoing basis, the next step is to determine how you ensure that the classroom contract remains "alive" for the students. We recommend creating an anchor chart of all of the classroom contracts that will impact your room each day. Clearly label the key components and make them visible for all students in the room. If you have more than one classroom contract due to having multiple groups of students during the course of your day, make sure that the intended audience of each contract is clear.

Work with students to determine the best way to make sure that they are reminded of what they agreed to and how this will be reinforced. We suggest making sure that once students sign their classroom contract, they have a copy to keep at all times. This may include having a laminated copy taped to their desk, attaching their copy to the inside cover of their classroom notebook or textbook, or including it on their learning device.

Having a place where students can turn for their classroom contract agreements is half the battle in getting students to embrace implementation. Like purchasing a treadmill for your home that makes it more convenient to work out, convenience alone will not get you to exercise. You will be healthier by getting on the treadmill on a regular basis and committing to a plan to use it. The same goes for having a class "get in shape" with their agreements. Having the document is great but using the document is what is necessary.

The document must be used consistently before contentious topics are to be discussed. Students must be able to "live" the classroom contract in low-risk situations in order to use it successfully in high-risk situations. This will be discussed more in depth in Chapter 4, but for now it is important to pair the "placement" of the classroom contract with the "use" of the classroom contract. The classroom contract should be readily accessible and utilized often to ensure that it does not become background noise.

Referring to some or all of the agreements regularly must be part of the classroom culture that you build from day one. The classroom contract can be reread out loud every Monday to remind students of what is expected of them for the coming week. This may include the entire document, or students can identify certain agreements that they felt were an issue the previous week and focus on rereading those agreements with examples of what worked and did not work previously. The same can occur at the start of activities that focus on student conversations. Discuss what went well last time, what did not go well last time, and which agreements the class needs to focus on to improve.

This constant cycle of referring to the agreements and encouraging student reflection supports the building of the community that will be needed to be successful with the most contentious topics down the line. Continue to have students build on what has worked in the past while exploring ways to get better at what has not gone well. These reflections are not a time for judgement or shaming, but they are intended to bring the classroom contract to life by keeping it relevant in their everyday interactions. Only by "working out" with the agreements in place can we get into better "shape" to lean on the classroom contract when needed.

Affirmations

Affirmations are one place where we can lean on our classroom contract. Many of us may have experiences with affirmations related to a growth mindset when we were younger, but often those much needed affirmations tend to be in short supply in the older grades. We need positive interactions and to acknowledge the times when we uphold our agreements.

Students will come to your classroom with a variety of backgrounds, beliefs, and personalities. These differences will enrich the learning experiences of your students, but they are also the reason that disagreements can occur. Throughout this process of creating a culture it is important to affirm students for who they are and the work that they are doing, so remember to build affirmations into your planning and regular routines.

There are many reasons why students may see themselves in a negative light, and conversations about contentious topics may bring some of these reasons to the surface for a student. In Chapter 2 we talked about how some relevant topics are ones that students might relate to their own self-identity. Conversations about what other students think about topics like these might put students in a position to hear what others are saying and internalize them as negative thoughts about themselves. We must be clear to students that the differences they bring into our classroom are reasons for celebration even as others might have differing points of view. This is a prime example of why we choose to use the word *contentious* so that we can try to avoid a student feeling that something about them is *controversial*.

There are two ways we can use affirmation in the classroom. First, we can have a class mantra such as, "Classroom discourse makes stronger communities." It may feel silly at first to secondary students, but over time, they will likely take it on as part of their classroom identity. Involve students in developing the mantra, just as you did with the class agreements.

The second way is to make positive affirmations a regular part of debriefing class discourse. Make it a routine to ask students to affirm ways in which they followed the class contract. At the end of any class discussion, invite students to state the positive aspects of the discourse—for example, "I affirm (student name) for listening to diverse points of view and seeking to understand them." You may need to model one or two times after conversations in class so that students understand what it looks like. As former high school teachers, we have seen firsthand the power of these positive interactions for students of this age; once they were able to get over the initial idea, they were able to articulate affirmations without teacher cues.

STOP TO THINK AND PREDICT

We've all heard stories about teachers who were attacked on social media or even placed on administrative leave due to an instructional choice in their classrooms (Stunson, 2021). While this risk can never be completely eliminated, we can be proactive and consider all the ways that our choices might be interpreted. The solution is not to shy away from anything that can be considered contentious, but instead to think ahead and be prepared for what might go wrong.

Teachers who establish a strong relationship with students, parents, and administrators have already taken a giant, foundational step toward preventing negative reactions to their instructional choices. Importantly, when planning a contentious conversation in the classroom, consider the different ways words, topics, and instructional strategies might be interpreted from a variety of perspectives.

For instance, if we are discussing an issue related to climate change in a community where many families work for the oil and gas industry, we should consider how some families may feel about the topic. Or if we are a white teacher preparing to discuss race, how might some of the students and their families interpret the words we choose to use or place on the board or instructional materials?

Anticipating the needs of students can also go a long way in strengthening the relationships that are present in the classroom as well as support student learning. The WIDA English Language Development Standards Framework was developed to support multilingual learners, but their application supports all students in your classroom. The Wisconsin Center for Education Research has developed six teacher discourse moves (2017a) and seven student discourse moves (2017b) that allow for students to better express their thoughts in conversation. Scan the QR codes to gain access to these moves.

Scan this QR code to access the Wisconsin Center for Education Research's teacher discourse moves.

Scan the QR code to access the Wisconsin Center for Education Research's student discourse moves.

After your classroom contract is complete and you start to think ahead to predict future challenges, incorporating some of the discourse moves is a great place to make sure that all of your students feel supported as well as to bring needed skills to all of your students. One example is the student discourse move of "restate or summarize." If there is a classroom contract agreement to "be good listeners," this can be reinforced by having a protocol in place that before a student speaks, they must first restate or summarize what was said by the previous student.

There are multiple benefits to the addition of this simple discourse move. On the surface, it helps to make sure that students are listening to what is being said as opposed to just waiting for their turn to speak. It also provides an opportunity to make sure that what a student said was interpreted by others in the manner in which it was intended. Once student A finishes speaking, student B would have to restate or summarize what student A said. After student B has given their restate-or-summarize statement, student A has the opportunity to agree that student B's statement was accurate and if not, then student A can clarify. Ensuring that student A was understood before student B continues the conversation helps to avoid misunderstanding. Adding this element to classroom norms can be one way to support student agreements while avoiding predicted issues related to misunderstandings due to student speaking and listening. This is just one example of how predicting the needs of some students can lead to integrating best practices that support implementation of classroom contracts.

TIPS FOR WORKING WITH ADMINISTRATORS AND FAMILIES

To have effective conversations, your class "community" must extend beyond your students. Parents and administrators should understand how situations and conversations happen in your classroom. We have created a list of tips to aid you in bringing administrators and families into your classroom.

1. **Open-door policy.** Invite parents into your classroom either in person or virtually. Technology allows parents to have a look into what is going on in your classroom. A regularly updated class website with access to lesson plans and student discussion boards lets parents know exactly what is going on in your classroom. The open-door policy lets administrators and parents know that the classroom is their room as well. Parents and administrators are able to view norms, know the syllabus, and are aware that they are free to come and participate whenever they have the time. Most parents

and administrators are busy with their daily lives, but knowing that they have access to your class is reassuring.

2. **Teacher–parent agreement.** Provide ways for parents to be aware of the goals you have for the class this year. Send home your agreement to show parents how the class will remain respectful and thoughtful during classroom discourse. Let parents know the intentions and goals you have from their students as well as expectations. Allow parents to personalize the agreement with any assurances they may need that are individual to their student. This agreement can be as simple as a letter home or a Google form for parents to check that they agree to support your learning environment.

3. **Frequent communication.** This is an area of weakness for many. Overcommunicate your expectations, agreements, and plans.

    a. Parents receive a mountain of information for their child from kindergarten to fifth grade. From sixth grade onward, the communication minimizes by the year. Information should still be consistent in the secondary instructional years. For instance, make parents aware that the class will be starting a unit about immigration and will look at graphic images and firsthand accounts. This allows parents to be prepared or ready to further discuss topics with their children. Consider providing a tip sheet of things parents can reinforce at home as it relates to civil discourse. Class newsletters are a great way to keep parents and guardians abreast of what is going on in the classroom. The class newsletter can be quarterly, monthly, or every grading period. The teacher should provide the following in the newsletter: their contact information, units being covered, assessments coming up, and things to do at home. You may also consider sending home a permission slip for students to cover and discuss sensitive topics in class. If parents "opt out," please remember to find an alternative option that still highlights the skills you want taught for the day and with a different topic.

b. Administrators should be in the know at all times. At the beginning of the year, provide your administrator two things:

   i. **A detailed course syllabus.** This course syllabus can be similar to what was given to parents as long as themes or units are explained in a little more detail so your administrator can have talking points if anyone has an issue.

   ii. **The dates of your classroom contract procedural day and signing day.** Even if your administrator is unable to attend, it allows them to see the seriousness of your efforts to provide an equitable, noncontroversial environment for students.

The best way to avoid issues is to make sure that your administrator knows what is going on in your classroom. General expectations around providing lesson plans and participating in professional learning communities (PLCs) in your school about topics and practices are a great start, but this may not be enough for your administrator to tackle any issues that may arise after a class. When conversations or topics are up for discussion that you know will cause some attention, your administrator should be made aware. This process is fairly easy if you invite your administrator to see the classroom contract procedure as well as the classroom contract signing, as then they would be well aware of the processes and procedures in your classroom.

Laying this solid foundation is critical before beginning discourse on contentious topics. Once students, administrators, and parents are all on the same page regarding the goals, policies, procedures, and protocols, we can begin practicing the skills of discourse with completely safe, nonemotional topics, which we will explore in Chapter 4.

CLOSING REFLECTION

- How will you respond when the unexpected happens?
- What policies need to be non-negotiable in your classroom?
- What can you do to help students take ownership of the responsibilities of the classroom?
- Why is building a sense of community and family necessary to address contentious topics?
- How do you adjust for the realities of the lives of your students when it comes to particular issues that relate to your community?

Now that you have read this chapter, you should be able to complete the following:

- ✓ Develop protocols for how to handle inappropriate comments and untimely questions in your classroom in order to know how you will react when the unexpected happens.
- ✓ In accordance with school and district policies, create a list of non-negotiable student agreements for your classroom.
- ✓ Identify places in your classroom where student voice and input can be included in the development of classroom agreements.
- ✓ Explore ways to get to know your students and their home lives as well as the values and traditions of the school and community.
- ✓ Collect examples of classroom agreements for students to examine when developing their own.
- ✓ Create a plan for how classroom agreements will be posted, reinforced, and communicated with administrators and parents.

CHAPTER 4

Empathy

Prepare With Safe Topics

Plan your work for today and every day, then work your plan.

—Margaret Thatcher

This chapter will help to prepare you to complete the following:

- ✓ Determine which skills are most essential for your students to develop.
- ✓ Co-create success criteria for what these skills look like with your students.
- ✓ Select noncontentious topics for students to practice the skills of discourse.
- ✓ Use structures, resources, and activities that support discourse skill development.

The priorities for the first few days of school are to build community and establish the protocols, procedures, and policies that will set the foundation for civil discourse. Now, we are ready to move toward building discourse skills with safe or noncontentious topics. Students will be ready for contentious discourse in time, but for now, we need students to practice the art of discourse and develop empathy. The success of the contentious conversations will rest heavily on everything that you have equipped your students with in the days between day one and the day of the contentious conversation. This chapter will help you lay out the map for you and your students as that journey begins.

Take a moment and reflect on the following questions:

- What does the ideal classroom discourse look like? How can that be modeled for your students?
- How do you want students to engage with one another when they disagree?
- Do you have different expectations of your students when the conversation is a more open-ended discussion compared to a structured debate? How do you communicate those expectations to your students?
- What do you hope students take away from conversations in your classroom to use in conversations with family and community members?

PERSPECTIVE MATTERS

The parable of the blind men and the elephant is a well-known story of perception (Peace Corps, n.d.). In summary, the story is about six blind men reaching out and all touching different parts of an elephant. Based on what the men feel (leg, ear, trunk, tusk, side, tail), they all have vastly different ideas about the animal that they are describing. As they share what they believe the animal to be, this leads to an argument about what an elephant is, what it does, and what it looks like. Since each man has only a small piece of information about an elephant, their "version" of the elephant is incomplete and inaccurate. Only by sharing what they know with each other are they able to fully "construct" the elephant. Ayo Magwood, founder of Uprooting Inequity, builds off of this parable to remind us that "perspective matters and it doesn't mean that you are wrong, but know that your own perspective is not universal" (Stern & Aleo, 2020).

The idea that two people can have two different perspectives and both be correct is highlighted in Figures 4.1 through 4.4. Are there three or four sticks in Figure 4.1? Is the number on the ground in Figure 4.2 a number six or a number nine? Figure 4.3 shows us that we can even see and recognize the same things but have different perspectives on their value depending on our individual situations—are you trying to get off the island or off the boat? In the complex realities of today's world, Figure 4.4 shows us that sometimes there are even more than two sides or perspectives to an idea.

FIGURE 4.1 Four or Three?

Illustration by Honore Schmidt

FIGURE 4.2 Six or Nine?

Illustration by Honore Schmidt

FIGURE 4.3 Boat or Land?

Illustration by Honore Schmidt

FIGURE 4.4 Circle, Triangle, or Square?

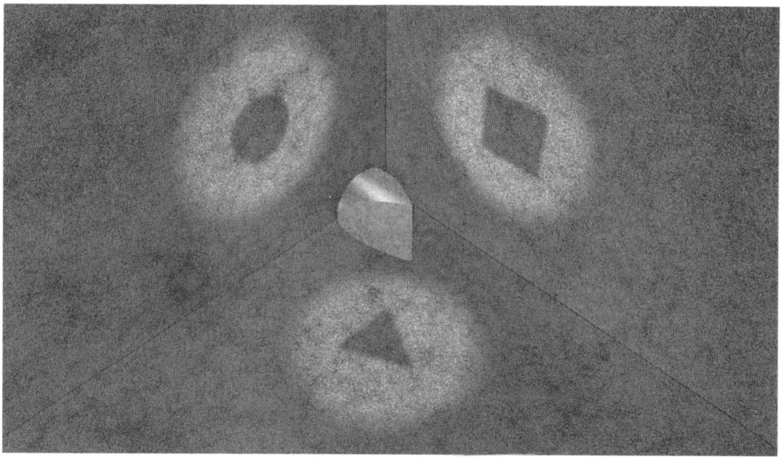

oscardamen (pixabay.com)

Professor Sam Wineburg, founder of the Stanford History Education Group, has spent the better part of 25 years exploring how we learn history. His work has led to a push to examine history and our contemporary world through multiple lenses of diverse, and often conflicting, primary sources. The use of primary sources is essential in terms of exploring information from multiple points of view in order to engage in historical thinking. One key premise of historical thinking is the idea that there is no one story that we can point to as the "correct" version of history. Instead of focusing on the absolute "correct" answer, our first goal should be to better understand that all of us, like the blind men touching the elephant, are only contributing one perspective to the story that will form the entire narrative of our history.

When students have to examine an issue from multiple perspectives, not only do they get a more complete picture of the issue, but they also have to develop the understanding that conflicting ideas can coincide with each other. Accepting that there is not one "correct" answer allows an appreciation of the nuanced layers of our history and ourselves. In this approach, students begin to see that our differences do not define us and can actually strengthen our historical understandings. None of us are as smart as all of us, and therefore, the best historical approach is always one that involves as many perspectives as possible.

In her 2009 TED Talk "The Danger of a Single Story," novelist Chimamanda Ngozi Adichie explains why we cannot hear one version of a story and accept it as the sole truth: "The single story creates stereotypes, and the problem with stereotypes is not that they are untrue, but that they are incomplete. They make one story become the only story." The danger of the single story extends beyond how we may view someone else through the lens of that single story. The danger of the single story is also directly related to the danger of only having conversations or reading sources that reinforce your beliefs. This creates incomplete stereotypes that often then become the only version of our world that we know or accept.

IDENTIFY DISCOURSE SKILLS

Jay McTighe and Grant Wiggins (1998) created what they called *Understanding by Design*, which focuses on the idea of backward planning to achieve results for student understanding (Authentic Education, 2015; Bowen, 1970). The three stages of backward planning are (1) identify desired results, (2) determine acceptable evidence, and (3) plan learning experiences and instruction. Many educators are familiar with Understanding by Design (UbD) and incorporate backward planning when either developing their curriculum or working to flesh out district- or state-approved curriculum. Here, we start with UbD as a way to get our students to the end result of the "ideal classroom conversation" that you pondered at the start of this chapter.

There are some generally accepted ideas about what the ideal classroom conversation should look like. See the examples listed in Figure 4.5.

FIGURE 4.5 Ingredients for the Ideal Classroom Conversation

Proper behavior and language use
Waiting your turn to speak/not interrupting
Eye contact with active listening
No side conversations
Listening for content
Responding to a statement directly without attacking the speaker
Finding common ground
Following the direction of the discussion
Asking appropriate clarifying questions
Differentiating between facts, opinions, and generalizations
Using reliable/valid sources to support claims

Source: Adapted from Street Law Inc. (2021) and U.S. Courts (n.d.).

While we might have been quick to list many of these characteristics, that is only the first step in planning supports. Many classrooms do not then take the time to scaffold these skills like we would do with students trying to learn how to read, write, or do multiplication. But they are skills that take time and practice to develop.

Like all skills we want our students to improve, we need to identify the end goal first so that we can determine what we would want from our students as evidence that they are able to do the skills. Some of these skills are fairly straightforward, such as "no side conversations" and "waiting your turn to speak/not interrupting." Other skills are more complex and this is where we sometimes struggle to support students. What does it mean for a student to demonstrate that they are "listening for content" or "finding common ground"? Even though the idea of "asking appropriate clarifying questions" sounds simple, veteran teachers know that many students struggle to do this without explicit instruction. What about trying to determine if each student is "differentiating between facts, opinions, and generalizations" in the moment that a statement is made?

When it comes to determining the acceptable evidence that students should be able to produce, there is nobody more qualified than the teachers of individual schools. This evidence will vary widely based on the grade level, the context of the learning, and how much experience the students have had with these skills. We have collected some examples of rubrics and success criteria for consideration (see the QR code), but we strongly encourage both classroom teachers and those developing district curriculum to spend time developing the success criteria that best align with the grade level of the classroom and the skills that best align with the long-term vision of the district.

Scan the QR code for examples of rubrics and success criteria.

Finally, we must align the skills with instruction and assessment. Discourse skills are more than a one-time learning activity or seen as an add on. We frequently work with teachers who agree that students should be able to "close-read primary sources to answer a document-based question," but they often resort to low-level, fact-based multiple-choice tests that do not align with that outcome. This disconnect is the problem that we must avoid in all facets of education, and working on communication skills should be no different.

SCAFFOLDING TOPICS

When we are talking about teaching the most difficult educational skills with students, we often use the analogy of teaching someone to drive a car. Too often in education, we keep the most advanced skills on a pedestal until we believe a student has reached the proper grade level in which to begin engaging with the learning. That is the equivalent of never having a teenager see or ride in a car until they are 16 years old, because before that they are "not able" to drive the car. Like exposure to riding in a car before driving the car, students can "take a ride" in conversations about contentious topics well before they are "driving the car."

Now that the outcome has been defined and the appropriate skills necessary to meet that outcome have been identified, it is time to practice. In order for students to grow in their skills related to engaging in conversations about contentious topics, students must get multiple opportunities to practice them. Like students doing multiplication with increasingly large numbers and reading texts of increasing difficulty, we must identify the necessary skills and allow students to practice with increasingly difficult structures and topics.

Students can be given opportunities to have their voices heard and share differing opinions without it actually being a debate about a contentious topic. Before students participate in structured formal debates or even discussions, they can still contribute to ideas on how to answer questions (e.g., "What should we do in the classroom since recess has been canceled?" or "What should we name the classroom goldfish?"). These are examples of things where a final decision will be reached after students share ideas and many of them will share ideas that end up not being the final decision. We cannot stress enough that while the most contentious topics and the most structured debates are not likely to show up in an elementary classroom, the skills necessary to do the work should be started in the elementary classroom well before students are having their most difficult conversations.

When working with middle and high school classrooms, the same opportunities need to be provided to students who may not have had any practice before they reached their current classroom. In the absence of a clear development path of these skills, make sure that formative assessments are being used to check in on student skill and ability level before jumping into the most layered structures involving the most contentious topics. "Like any other skill, the ability to engage in civil discourse requires practice. Don't expect students to get it right the first time, and don't expect them to be able to start with highly controversial topics right off the bat" (National Council for the Social Studies, n.d.).

Like the analogy of teaching someone to drive a car, it is probably still best to scaffold the learning. When someone is driving for the very first time, we would not advise you to give them a Ferrari and have them jump on the highway to drive cross country alone, regardless of how many hours they have spent riding in a car or how many books they have read about driving a car. What most, if not all, new drivers go through when learning to drive starts in a driveway, with us making sure that the new driver knows where all of the buttons are and what they do. New drivers then "graduate" to driving slowly down a barely used back road or empty parking lot. Parking takes place between the lines with no other cars next to that spot so that if the lines are missed, no cars are damaged. After new drivers demonstrate the ability to properly use all of the buttons and pedals, they head out onto the road with traffic for the first time *with* supervision and support. Traditionally then, hours are tracked and certain skills are practiced until they reach the point of being ready to take their road test for their license.

These formative check-ins on driving skills in preparation for the road test take on the same approach that should be used with students who will someday take the "final exam" of talking about a highly contentious topic. To help minimize the number of "car accidents" that the student is involved in, formative check-ins on student skill and ability should focus on topics that, while contentious, would not be considered controversial or even political. We want to find topics that are engaging but otherwise have a low emotional temperature. Table 4.1 provides some examples of introductory topics that can be used as early as elementary school that allow students to practice their skills.

TABLE 4.1 Introductory Questions (Elementary Friendly)

- Which is the best flavor of ice cream? Chocolate or vanilla?
- What would you rather have as a treat? Cookies or candy?
- Which makes a better pet? Puppies or kittens?
- What is the correct way to cut a sandwich? Diagonal or perpendicular?
- What is the best season? Fall or spring?

It is important to start with introductory questions because they are focused almost exclusively on people's personal preferences. When it comes to providing "evidence" of your choice, a lot of it will be personal opinion instead of empirical data, though researching the sales of the different choices would support valuable research skills that will be necessary as the topics get more contentious. Since the evidence is more about opinion, this means that if "my side" loses, it is far easier to accept because I can still order chocolate ice cream that evening or ask my parents for a puppy even if everyone in my class disagrees. Even the youngest of children can be helped to understand that people have different "favorites" and that is okay.

The introductory topics might seem to be a waste of time with older students, but they allow students a place to practice some of the most basic conversational skills necessary to participate in more contentious issues down the line. If you have older students or want your students to dig a little deeper into their thinking when they start, we would still advise against using the political issues of the day and instead first think about some of topics that focus more on a yes-or-no answer that has to be backed up with a bit more substance than "because it is my favorite."

TABLE 4.2 Moderate Questions

- Which came first? The chicken or the egg?
- Does money buy happiness?
- Is hard work more important than talent?
- Does the internet make people smarter?
- Does a straw have one hole or two?

Whatever skills you believe are absolutely necessary for students to have and use during the most contentious conversation must be practiced and reinforced in the classroom throughout the year. Topics and questions, like the moderate questions found in Table 4.2, can be practiced with students who already have some experience with classroom conversations. Again, these are your students driving the car at 5 mph in an open parking lot or parallel parking between cones. If something is going to go wrong while scaffolds are still necessary, make sure you are using topics and questions that elicit more laughter than anger.

There are plenty of questions that will get students emotionally engaged that are still a step away from politically contentious issues that may lead to parent phone calls. Once students have been exposed to the different ways that conversations will happen in the classroom (remember the 3Ds), we would suggest a couple rounds of discussion and debate about some pop culture "controversies" before tackling the politically charged content topics. Table 4.3 includes some "advanced" questions we have used with students that have led to animated engagement worthy of the time.

TABLE 4.3 Advanced Questions

- Is a hot dog a sandwich?
- Is it okay to put pineapple on pizza?
- Is cereal with milk a soup?
- Should the toilet paper roll hang over or under?
- Are fake Christmas trees better than real ones?

By the time you are using questions like the advanced questions, students should be expected to follow all of the rules of engagement regardless of the conversation structure. This includes not only how they speak and react to and with each other, but also the more complicated skills of how to clearly state their claim and use appropriately cited evidence to show thoughtful reasoning.

Many of the sample questions in this chapter are adapted from the board game *I Dissent: A Game of Supreme Opinions* (Buffalo Games, 2020), which does a great job of capturing 81 light-hearted "hot-button" issues of today. It is important to keep in mind that the scaffolding of the questions does not have to be fun noncontent-specific questions. When planning ahead in order to scaffold practicing the skills, the focus should be on finding questions that will allow students to keep their emotions at a level that will allow them to stay focused on the skills and procedures. The issue that we are trying to avoid is when the procedures of the conversation break down in a manner that leads to emotional reactions that override the skills that should be the focus. The idea that "whoever speaks loudest and longest wins" is one that takes time to overcome. Check out the QR code for additional resources and topics.

Scan the QR code for additional conversation resources and topics.

This type of scaffolding related to question and skill complexity is similar to how we teach students most other intellectual skills, including mathematics, reading, and writing. When it comes to having conversations, it is common to assume that since we talk to each other all of the time, we must have a basic understanding of the rules and skills necessary to participate. By building a progression of questions and skills, this allows students to practice the skills in a safe way and gives teachers plenty of opportunities to formatively assess students. Like other skills, when teachers identify gaps in student learning and understanding related to these skills, targeted support specific to the skill(s) is necessary. When you have contentious topics in your curriculum that must be addressed and have identified the skills necessary for students to have those conversations, be sure to build in layers of questions that allow for the students to "test drive" what you expect of them, before they hit the open road.

BUILDING BACKGROUND KNOWLEDGE

There is a lot of research that tells us one of the biggest indicators in a student's ability to read is their background knowledge (Knowledge Matters Campaign, 2018). Dr. Robert Marzano has been pushing this as essential to a student's academic success since 2004, and O'Reilly et al. (2019) found where the "knowledge threshold" created a "barrier to comprehension." The importance of background knowledge is just as essential when it comes to having conversations about contentious topics.

In early October 2020, Joe wrote a blog urging teachers who planned on talking about the election on Election Day to start preparing immediately (Schmidt, 2020). Part of this was to set up the classroom culture and structures that have been discussed already in this book, and part of it was to make sure that students had the background knowledge necessary to have the discussions.

> Look for potential precedent and build background knowledge wherever you can. Are your students familiar with the *Bush v. Gore* Supreme Court case in 2000? What about how the Election of 1824 played out in Congress? Do they know how the Electoral College works? Spend time building as much background knowledge as you can when it comes to the information that students will most likely need to know in order to understand issues that may come up. (Schmidt, 2020)

If you anticipate that topics may get emotionally or politically charged, you need to be working from a strong foundation of background knowledge to help keep students grounded in accurate information that they can and should be using as part of the conversation that they are having.

The conversation that students will engage in in the classroom should be grounded in skills that support using what they know to process new information. When we are having conversations around contentious topics, especially in debate format, we do not want students trying to process new information on the spot. As discussed in Chapter 2, when we are preparing to have conversations rooted in policy, students must be given the information and data at least a day ahead of time to build their foundational knowledge. This is where the idea of planning for tomorrow is so important. Having students work with these topics with little advance support is setting them up to fail.

The contentious conversations that you're going to have in the classroom should be aligned to the key concepts, topics, and ideas of the course as a whole. If this is the case, there should be ample opportunity to make sure that students have a firm understanding of all of these concepts, topics, and ideas before talking with their peers regardless of the structure used. Keep in mind that the amount of background knowledge necessary for the conversation is dependent on the structure. The more collaborative the discussion, the more likely that students will use their peers as thought partners to help them better understand the topic. We believe that even at this level, the more background information students have at their disposal, the more they will gain from the conversation.

Background knowledge extends beyond information specific to the topic. As highlighted in Chapter 2, there are different sets of concepts that students need to understand and properly use in order to successfully participate in conversations in the classroom. In terms of practicing skills ahead of your most contentious conversations, students will need to know the difference between facts, opinions, and generalizations. They will need to know these differences in order to properly use them in classroom conversations but also in order to properly hear and understand what their classmates are saying.

While most of us, students included, know that we want to have our conversation grounded in facts, students will use opinions and generalizations as well. Take time to make sure that your students have a shared understanding of the definitions of *fact*, *opinion*, and *generalization*, as shown in Table 4.4.

TABLE 4.4 Definitions of Fact, Opinion, and Generalization

Fact	A true piece of information
Opinion	What someone thinks about a particular thing
Generalization	A general statement, law, principle, or proposition

SOURCE: Merriam-Webster (2021a).

Using a Frayer model (Figure 4.6), groups work to develop a shared understanding of a concept as they use the definition to list key characteristics, examples, and nonexamples. Once completed, the class can practice identifying facts, opinions, and generalizations in any conversation. Students should then be given the tools and opportunities to demonstrate that they can decipher between facts, opinions, and generalization in real-time conversations with their peers. In order to provide these tools and opportunities, we advise developing procedures to clear up any potential confusion.

FIGURE 4.6 Frayer Model

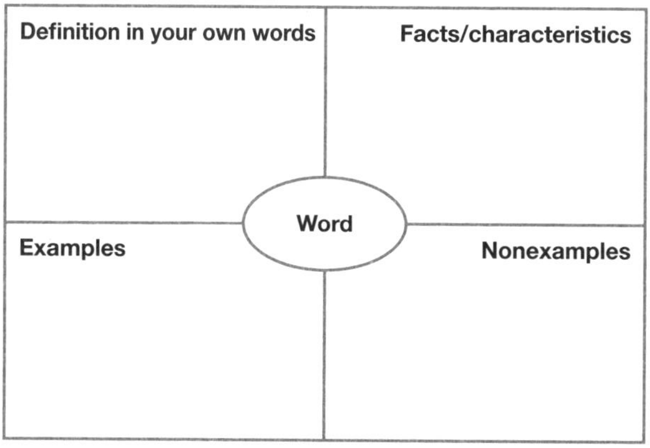

One procedure we suggest having in your classroom is the *FOG check*, where any student can call for a FOG check at any time. FOG refers to the first letter of the terms *facts*, *opinions*, and *generalizations*. Students should constantly be working to "clear the FOG" in all of their conversations. During a FOG check, the student would identify the statement that they want clarity on. Is it a fact, opinion, or generalization? The original speaker of the statement would provide a response to help clear the FOG, then classmates would share their thoughts about the statement before ending the FOG check. It is important to note that this is not intended for the speaker to defend their belief or for other students to challenge it, but rather it serves as an opportunity for students to hear what others are thinking about that idea to help build understanding. Students may likely feel defensive about a FOG check, so in most cases it is best to keep the focus on students hearing each other as opposed to reaching a definitive conclusion on its status as a fact, opinion, or generalization.

Students can practice clearing the FOG ahead of any conversation by doing close reads of any articles that you provide ahead of time. Facing History and Ourselves (n.d.) has a FOG Analysis worksheet for students that can be assigned for individual completion. Scan the QR code to view the FOG Analysis worksheet.

Scan the QR code to view the FOG Analysis worksheet.

Once completed, the class as a whole could compare responses to help bring a shared understanding of not only what was read but also in identifying the differences between facts, opinions, and generalizations. Scan the QR code to view a sample FOG Analysis.

Scan the QR code to view a sample FOG Analysis.

Another part of background knowledge that students will need to be successful in your classroom is understanding the structures you have in place and how they should navigate them. This is a component of classroom conversations that is often taken for granted but should be set up, practiced, and reinforced. For example, how are your students called on when they have something to say? Do they raise their hand and wait to be called on, or do you randomly call on students? Is there a form of educational technology being used to indicate when they are ready to speak or to record thoughts? Are there procedures in place to help monitor the air time of students? Is every student expected to speak at least once? Can they opt out of speaking, and are written responses acceptable as well? We are not advocating for one specific structure, rule, or educational technology over others; rather, we are reinforcing the idea of making sure that students have a clear understanding of how you will run the classroom and how they are expected to participate and communicate. Whatever the structures used in the classroom are, make sure to introduce them well in advance and to remain consistent with expectations throughout all student experiences.

SKILL-BUILDING STRUCTURES

Using consistent structures in the classroom goes well beyond students knowing how they will be called upon to speak and how often they are expected to participate. To this point, we have laid out everything that should be happening in your classroom from day one through and up to the actual conversation about the most contentious topics that will be addressed as part of your curriculum. Like structures in the daily routines of classrooms, bigger-picture structures are helpful in designing a safe place for student conversations to occur. Here are two final pieces to consider before we engage in discourse around contentious topics, described in the next chapter.

LETS ACT Framework

The LETS ACT Framework created by Genevieve Caffrey (n.d.) is a simple but powerful way to remember the key points and steps outlined in this book and is closely aligned with the best practices that support successful student conversations. Caffrey's model was included in *Social Education* as part of an article titled "A Pathway to Racial Literacy: Using the LETS ACT Framework to Teach Controversial Issues" (King et al., 2018) and was the center of a Visions of Education (2020) podcast. The framework consists of seven steps that help to guide educators as they work to create an environment to support student conversations about contentious topics, as shown in Figure 4.7.

FIGURE 4.7 LETS ACT Framework

L	Loving/Listen
E	Educate
T	Talk
S	Search
A	Analyze
C	Conclude
T	Take

The **L** in LETS ACT is about creating a "loving" environment where we "listen" to students and celebrate their personal backgrounds and experiences. We highlighted the importance of building this type of classroom culture throughout Chapter 3. Putting in the time at the beginning of the year to set the stage allows students to feel free to share and to be recognized as experts of their own experiences.

Once the teacher has created the environment in which students feel safe to share what they already know, the next step is to **E**ducate. This is where the students build background knowledge in the content subject area and are reminded of classroom protocols as discussed earlier in this chapter. The more familiarity students have with classroom routines and with the background knowledge of the topic, the more likely they are to be able to keep emotions at a level that will allow for respectful conversations. When discussing the most contentious topics, keep the number of variables that the students have to process at a minimum.

Students then come to the table to **T**alk, specifically in a format that is focused on sharing ideas. "Teachers can facilitate an interactive activity that allows students to talk about the issue in small groups in a way that does not force them to take a position on the issue—yet" (King et al., 2018). These activities allow students to participate in civil discourse by working with information and ideas with a relatively neutral stance. With more of a focus on collaboration (think dialogue and discussion) instead of competitiveness, this is an opportunity to bring in the collaborative side of the 3Ds discussed in Chapter 2. By providing these talk opportunities, students are able to engage in rich dialogue and discussion as they build background knowledge.

The idea of having students talk also aligns with starting students with data in a role in which the data are not up for debate. With the focus on collaboration, it becomes more clear to students that the data are shared to help build understanding, not to debate. Students can take multiple perspectives on a piece of data without having to take a stance that might put them in the position of saying something detrimental during the class conversation. An example of this type of activity is having students sort news articles based on pros/cons, political beliefs, values of the writer/speaker, and any other way that might be relevant for future conversations. As questions arise, this is the perfect opportunity for a discussion to see if the group can work together to find the answer. If the group feels more information is needed, encourage them to record their questions about what they know and still want to know.

Now that students have begun to think about and discuss the topic at hand, give them space to do a bit of exploration on their own. This is done through the Search and the Analyze stages of the LETS ACT Framework. During this time, students are starting to move toward taking a position on the issue at hand. They have engaged in civil discourse and built background knowledge as part of small groups, while hearing from others, developing questions, and exploring different perspectives. Now they look for additional information to answer the questions that developed during the Talk stage to bring back to the conversation. Practicing the skills of media literacy and research skills is key during this step. Based on the grade and skill level of your students, provide the support necessary to help them find answers to their questions.

Through this analysis, students prepare to participate in conversation that moves toward the competitive side of the 3Ds usually in the form of a formal discussion or debate where they will reach a conclusion. By engaging in dialogue with their peers, students are in a position to build their understanding of the ideas of others as they try to reach a consensus. Remember that not all topics are conducive to reaching a "winning" answer. When students Conclude, they may reach a conclusion based on a sharing of ideas (dialogue), as part of a group discussion, or one side may be declared the "winner" of a debate based on the strength and clarity of their argument. This step of LETS ACT is supported by the strategies identified in Chapter 5. Pay particular attention to how we suggest you GUIDE your students through the 3Ds of discourse strategies as you move from dialogue early in LETS ACT toward more debate types of discourse by the end. The GUIDE elements set the stage for successful classroom civil discourse. We will explore the GUIDE elements further in Chapter 5.

The LETS ACT Framework wraps up by having students Take action based on what they have learned. This does not necessarily mean that they will be supporting the conclusion reached by the class (if a "winning" answer is the result); rather, they will share what they have learned with others, aligned with dimension four of the C3 Framework (National Council for the Social Studies, 2017). "Taking informed action moves students beyond a discussion of the ways things are or should be and propels them forward as real stakeholders with power to influence political decisions in the public sphere" (King et al., 2018). While the last step gives the teacher another opportunity to evaluate student learning, it also gives students an opportunity to see how the importance of conversations like the one they just participated in extends beyond a classroom assignment.

Argument Mapping

Students can be supported as they move through the LETS ACT Framework by using argument maps. *Argument mapping* is another tool students can work with in order to better understand not only what their peers are saying but also how to more clearly structure their own thoughts. Most people are familiar with the idea of claims, evidence, and reasoning when it comes to building an argument. By using argument maps,

ThinkerAnalytix brings one more piece to the table by having students identify the claims involved as well. According to ThinkerAnalytix Chief Operating Office Nate Otey, "If we do not identify the premise in an argument this will oftentimes lead to us talking past one another" (Massachusetts Council for the Social Studies, 2018). This is because arguments rarely have one premise and sometimes have hidden premises that unless surfaced can magnify misunderstanding.

The goal of every social studies teacher is to help students become critical thinkers of historical information who can engage in authentic discourse about historical topics, contentious or otherwise. Argument mapping provides the window for this growth. Argument mapping is a visual representation of decision-making while building upon critical thinking skills. This idea originally stems from the research of Stephen Toulmin's method of argumentation that focuses on the breakdown of an argument (van der Brugge, 2018). Argument mapping pulls from this research and focuses on the conclusion first. From the conclusion, students create preferable claims that support the conclusion or main claim. The students also create additional support for the preferable options or claims. Each argument mapping activity encourages students to think about ways to look at alternative solutions and rely on information to make logical strong arguments.

Students can work on argument mapping to develop their conversation skills, especially in anticipation of your most contentious topics. The amount of time and practice your students have put into argument mapping up to this point will guide how you should best use this strategy at this time. Experienced argument mappers can work in real time to track what is being said, especially if students are instructed to clearly identify how their response fits with other statements. Students with less experience in argument mapping can still complete an argument map, which can be turned in and assessed in place of the oral conversations. This can be an effective practice for students who may feel ready to verbally engage in civil discourse.

Like the strategies that we identify in Chapter 5, argument mapping can be used as a specific classroom activity on the day of the conversation about a contentious topic, but argument mapping goes beyond a pedagogical strategy. "Argument mapping is a visual method of displaying how reasons work to support a claim. A map exposes the hidden structure of the argument so that everyone can see how all the reasons fit together" (ThinkerAnalytix, 2021). Breaking down this hidden structure is the key to understanding the argument, but the ability to successfully do so takes an ongoing commitment to making this part of your classroom learning.

The skills developed from argument mapping impact student learning on a variety of levels. Maralee Harrell's (2012) research concluded,

> We determined that the students did develop the skills in which we were interested over the course of the semester. We also determined that the students who were taught argument diagramming gained significantly more than the students who were not. We conclude that learning how to construct argument diagrams significantly improves a student's ability to analyze arguments. (p. 31)

Knowing that these arguments are often political, argument mapping can also change how those with political differences see each other. "Using highly polarizing stimuli, we found that argument visualization substantially reduced confirmation bias and, for participants with low CRT [cognitive reflection test] scores, the belief that one's political opponents are morally evil" (Cullen & Sharma, n.d.). The outcomes of argument mapping include better analysis of arguments, reduced confirmation bias, and seeing those whom we disagree with in a more positive light; these are worth the time and effort in your classroom.

Effective use of argument mapping takes time to develop so that students can effectively utilize all of its components. With argument mapping, students have to work through an argument by identifying premises, determining if evidence supports or refutes an idea, and examining how all of the pieces fit together both for and against a claim. "You can map objections to any premise, so you can see exactly where two people disagree. The process of mapping also exposes hidden assumptions (a.k.a. implicit co-premises), which are often the true source of disagreement" (ThinkerAnalytix, 2021).

Argument mapping can be used to prepare for a conversation, to track a conversation in real life, and to analyze a conversation that has already taken place. Research shows us that the process of argument mapping supports student writing as well. "The experimental results showed that the argumentative essays produced by the students in the argument map writing group were superior to those written by students in the other two groups" (Fan & Chen, 2021, p. 159). While many of us think of discourse and debates as spoken exchanges, it is important to remember that some students express themselves best in writing. This means that when addressing the most contentious topics, some students will need an opportunity to "speak" in written form in order to feel safe.

Identifying and using the tools and skills of argument mapping can be a great resource as part of your most contentious conversations. ThinkerAnalytix has scaffolded resources to isolate and practice these skills in advance. Not only does ThinkerAnalytix have a variety of puzzles and quizzes, but they also have a free online course that guides students in learning more about using argument mapping to identify and organize all of the information of a given claim (see https://thinkeranalytix.org).

While there are a variety of ways that students can prepare to have a conversation about a contentious topic, we believe it is important to plan ahead and develop a long-term plan. With a clear plan that starts well before the first potential "heated debate," you will have an opportunity to model what is expected of your students. With modeling comes exposure to your policies, protocols, and procedures that will be the foundation of successful conversations. With expectations and practice that reinforces these expectations, you are now ready to support students as they do the heavy lifting around the most contentious topics.

CLOSING REFLECTION

- What are the skills that you have identified that will be at the heart of the conversations that you and your students have in your classroom?
- What are the most contentious topics that will be addressed in your curriculum? What are some "low-stakes" topics that can be used to build skills in preparation?
- How will your most contentious topics be addressed ahead of time through the building of background knowledge aligned to standards, curriculum, and assessment?
- Why is it important for your students to have clear expectations about how to engage in conversations? What type of frameworks will you use to model these expectations?

Now that you have read this chapter, you should be able to complete the following:

- ✓ Determine which skills are most essential for your students to develop.
- ✓ Co-create success criteria for what these skills look like with your students.
- ✓ Select noncontentious topics for students to practice the skills of discourse.
- ✓ Use structures, resources, and activities that support discourse skill development.

CHAPTER 5

Discourse

Structures for Contentious Topics

Was the American Revolution a fight against tyranny or an attempt by the well bred to maintain their social status? Was the Cold War really a conflict of democracy versus communism or a struggle between two superpowers for dominance? Divergent opinions swirl around these questions and other matters of unsettled history—opinions that get students talking, and thinking, and learning.

—Sam Wineburg (2010)

This chapter will help to prepare you to complete the following:

- ✓ Design your classroom to support successful student participation in civil discourse.
- ✓ Identify strategies that you will implement in your classroom when discussing contentious topics.

(Continued)

(Continued)

- ✓ Determine which contentious topics of your curriculum best align with each of those strategies.
- ✓ Identify what strategies will work best with your students based on grade level.
- ✓ Make a plan for how you will respond when something goes wrong while students are engaging in discourse.

What better hope could we have for our students than to get them "talking, and thinking, and learning"? And if "divergent opinions" are the way to get them to this learning, then we must not shy away from supporting them in this endeavor. Today is the day that you have been planning for. Today is the day that your students will engage in an activity related to one of the most contentious topics that they will discuss all year. Luckily for them, they have a teacher who has not taken this task lightly. You have read this book so that you are better prepared to support your students and you have put in the time and effort to set the stage for this conversation. Today, your students will be successful because of everything that you have done to get them to this point.

Take a moment and reflect on the following questions:

- Have you developed a classroom culture where students have demonstrated an ability to engage with one another?
- Are the policies, protocols, and procedures of your class clear and have they become routine for students?
- Do your students know the skills that they are working on and how you are defining success with those skills?
- Are your students equipped with the background knowledge necessary to engage with the topic at hand?
- What are the steps of your favorite pedagogical strategy that you will be using for your conversation today?

GENERAL STRUCTURES FOR SUCCESS

Previous chapters have laid the foundation for a positive classroom culture, strong communication with administrators and parents, and skills development for civil discourse. There are a few more pieces to consider before actually engaging in the contentious conversation. They include critical discourse elements we call GUIDE, grouping considerations, and concept attainment.

GUIDE

Now we are ready for civil discourse on the thorny issues that must be discussed in a healthy, thriving democracy. The following elements should be present for every conversation on contentious topics. Conveniently, they spell out the word GUIDE for ease in remembering them.

- **Guiding Question:** An overarching question (or motion, in the case of debate) provides a focus for discourse. In dialogue and discussion, it should be an open-ended question with no definitive right or wrong answer, but one that requires strong reasoning and evidence to answer. In debates, there is usually a motion and students argue for and against adoption of the motion. The question or motion shows students that the conversation will stay on track and they can keep referring back to it during the discourse.
- **Uninterrupted Thinking Time:** Students should be given individual time to think about the guiding question. If we've laid the foundation by building background knowledge using the structures found in Chapter 4, three to five minutes for individual thought gathering might be enough; this is where teachers' discretion will come into play. It helps to provide an organizational tool to jot down initial thoughts and ideas. This organizational tool

is not to be graded or seen by others, but it serves as a way for students to arrange what they are thinking. Scan the QR code for organizational tool ideas and templates.

Scan this QR code for organizational tool ideas and templates.

- **Information Provided:** Provide unbiased, concise information on the general topic such as charts, data, infographics, short summaries, or video clips. This information should give enough detail that your least prepared student can still participate authentically. Allow students time to go through the information. There are many resources available, such as PBS NewsHour Extra, ProCon.org, and Allsides.com, that provide concise information and multiple perspectives on current events.
- **Dedicated Q&A Time:** Give students time to ask clarifying questions before the discourse begins. Allowing students time for questions helps them feel comfortable to explore different perspectives and possibilities. Strategies such as an anonymous Padlet, sticky notes, or index card activities give students a safe place to answer burning questions without the spotlight being on any particular student.
- **Exit Opportunity:** Students need to know that if a topic or question is just "too much," they can opt out. This is one of the most important parts of the process. Knowing that it is okay to sit back and watch or go do something else during a discourse on a contentious topic gives students the option to self-regulate if needed and take a pause.

Grouping Considerations

As educators we attend professional learning sessions in which we are required to interact with "strangers" constantly. In those environments, presenters provide opportunities for us to get to know one another. Even with this time it is rare that we fully open up to our newfound colleagues. This experience is similar to our students except the adolescent dramas of life can change the climate of your class daily. When discussing contentious topics in class, we encourage teachers to be mindful of groupings. Take into account student experiences and readiness levels. Allow groups to work together for at least a unit before switching them. This will allow for students to discuss more in depth.

According to Bruce W. Tuckman's (1965) studies of group development, each group goes through five stages: forming, storming, norming, performing, and adjourning. Allowing your groups to go through the stages will provide optimal opportunities for students to grow.

Assigning vs. Self-Selection vs. Self-Selection Flipping

When it comes to a particular stance or position on a contentious topic, we can (1) assign students a particular "side" or "stance" to take, (2) let them select their stance, or (3) let them select their stance while also finding a few arguments for the opposing side.

There are pros and cons to these different approaches, as shown in Table 5.1.

Let's look at how all approaches can be used with a topic in an early United States History course. For instance, the guiding questions could be: In what ways was the Westward Expansion of the United States positive? And in what ways was it negative?

TABLE 5.1 Pros and Cons

APPROACH	PROS	CONS
Assigning	Students are encouraged to look at issues from a perspective that they would normally not choose.	Students might have a difficult time arguing a view opposite of what they actually believe.
Self-selection	Students are invested in the topic.	Students pick topics based on friends and what is currently trending. If the vast majority of the class feels a certain way, it may not be much of a discourse.
Self-selection flipping	Students are invested in the topic and they have to at least consider what an opposing view would be for the topic.	Students may not give the opposing view enough effort and only superficially search for opposing arguments.

Assigning

Students are given a perspective through which to explore the idea of Manifest Destiny. They look for evidence to support their assigned perspective or position that would intentionally bring diverse perspectives to the table regardless of the diversity of the classroom.

Self-Selection

Students can be given the opportunity to approach the topic from the viewpoint that is most appealing to them. Having the information or description available to make an educated selection is important. This example can be taken a step further and students can decide if they want to discuss Manifest Destiny or current immigration policies in their area. Both of these topics will still yield students the skills needed to understand the concepts we need them to capture from the unit.

Self-Selection Flipping

Have your students prepare for the debate by completing what's called a 5-3-1 for an "entry slip." This means that students come to class prepared to argue for one side of the topic. In order to physically step into the classroom, students have to show their entry-slip notes that include the following:

- Five supporting arguments for their side
- Three supporting arguments for the other side
- One question they anticipate the other side asking them

The 5-3-1 strategy has students look into both sides of an argument and anticipate a potential question from the other side. This reinforces the idea that in order to be prepared for a debate, one must be familiar with both sides of the argument. It also allows the teacher to "flip" the sides of the debate and have students argue for the "other side." This is a good strategy when students say they do not know what to say for the side that they did not pick. It is also a helpful way to reframe a conversation that extended beyond the first day, as a new 5-3-1 entry slip allows for new ideas and perspectives to be highlighted than those covered the first day.

Each option allows students to explore the information and provide responses that yield to students' understanding the contentious topic further. Each approach should be utilized in class.

Also, when thinking about grouping, keep your intended outcomes in mind. Initial research from McAvoy and McAvoy (2021) showed that the grouping of students can play a role in how they are impacted by the classroom conversations. The researchers surveyed students for the strength of their beliefs on political issues to form a baseline. They then found that when students were grouped in smaller groups with the intent to reach a consensus about the "best" solution to a problem, student beliefs about the issues moderated and they moved closer together compared to the original baseline spectrum. Conversely, when students worked in large groups in a debate format to reach a "winner" of a best solution to a problem, student beliefs about the issues became strengthened and they moved further apart compared to the original baseline spectrum. With this in mind, work to do grouping in a way that aligns with your goals.

We are not advocating that the goal should be to achieve one particular result over another; rather, we want educators to understand that grouping students for intended outcomes does impact what students take away from classroom conversations. In their research for *The Political Classroom*, Hess and McAvoy (2014) found that students with stronger opinions about political issues were more likely to vote after leaving high school. So while educators often want students to moderate strong stances, this may actually contradict another educator goal of getting students to become engaged voters.

Concept Attainment

Some may argue that access to unreliable information online can sometimes cripple students' abilities to have genuine and authentic intellectual conversations. In recent years, the overwhelming amount of misinformation and the political mudslinging displayed on the internet have made it so we are not all "speaking the same language." For instance, words like *communism*, *socialism*, and *totalitarianism* are often used interchangeably to describe opposing political parties. But these terms are not the same and are not completely open to interpretation. There are definitions of these terms, which can ensure everyone is referring to the same idea in the same way rather than talking in circles.

Concepts are important to understand the world we live in, and embracing them makes social studies instruction easier

(Stern et al., 2021). Introducing disciplinary concepts prior to the instruction of a contentious topic helps students look at the topic from similar lenses. Concepts such as privacy, alliances, authority, rule of law, and role and size of government are all essential for most contentious conversations.

For example, a United States government course might discuss this question: What is students' right to privacy in schools? Before jumping into famous court cases such as *Tinker v. Des Moines Independent School District* (1969), *New Jersey v. T.L.O.* (1985), and *Hazelwood School District v. Kuhlmeier* (1988), we need to explore the concepts of rights and privacy first. To acquire these concepts, students should be able to answer the following:

- What is a right? What is privacy?
- What are examples of rights? What are examples of privacy?
- What do privacy and rights look like at home vs. at school?
- Does everyone have rights? Does everyone have privacy?

After exploring the concepts and creating a common language of what they are, students can then explore the court cases with a base level of understanding. Students will then attempt to connect the concepts and similarities of each court case. Now students can respond and discuss the question: Should students have the right to privacy no matter their age and location?

SPECIFIC DISCOURSE STRATEGIES

This section is a short list of some of our favorite "day of" pedagogical strategies. We have used these strategies in our own classrooms and with other educators with great success, and we encourage you to give them a try. It is important for students to gain an understanding of the procedures of these strategies in combination with your expectations about how they should be incorporated in your classroom, and this will take some practice. With that in mind, we list eight seven strategies but suggest that you focus on only a couple during a given school year with your students. This approach allows you to get comfortable with the necessary facilitation steps and gives students the opportunity to focus on the learning as opposed to the "step-by-step" procedures. Remember that students can focus on the *how to do* or the *what I'm learning*, but trying to do both at the same time will reduce the effectiveness of both and could potentially lead to issues.

Talk Moves and Can of Worms

Students need to understand how to disagree with others respectfully. As we set the tone for discourse, it is imperative that initially we give students the words to say to guide those discussions. We all know the importance of sentence stems for English language learners, but they are a great resource to help guide discussions and questions for students. The Talk Moves and Can of Worms approaches give students various ways to enter conversations, deepen the discussion, and transition the thinking over the topics being discussed.

For instance, these Talk Moves sentence stems (the 3Cs of Thought) can assist students in organizing and sharing their thoughts. Students share their thinking by starting with one of the following:

- What ______ said CHALLENGED my thinking by/because . . .
- What ______ said CHANGED my thinking by/because . . .
- What ______ said CONFIRMED my thinking by/because . . .

With the Can of Worms approach, the following sentence starters can be used to further the conversation and help students learn to justify why they agree or disagree.

- I agree with ______ but ______.
- That's a good point but ______.
- I disagree with your ideas of ______ and I think ______.

Not only do all of these sentence stems give students three different ways to organize their thoughts about what they are hearing, but they also emphasize the idea that the goal is not to change someone else's mind. It is possible that someone may have their mind changed by what they hear, but it is more likely that someone will be "challenged" about their thinking before they change their mind. There is also the option to have one's thinking "confirmed" by what they hear, which gives students an opportunity to build off of that thought.

The 3Cs of Thought can be used to build background knowledge of a topic when students are preparing for a classroom activity. Consider using an entry slip where students come to class prepared by completing the 3Cs of Thought sentence stems about an assigned reading(s) or independent research about the topic. These three different ways of approaching information push students to look beyond confirming what they believe and look for ideas that also change or challenge their thinking. With the idea that "changed thinking" might not be common, the changed thinking will most likely need to be framed around how what they learned changed their thinking about a specific person, place, detail, and so on, as opposed to moving from one side of the argument to another. Changing thinking about some parts of a contentious topic is a way to help bring people together who still fundamentally disagree about the big picture.

While the 3Cs of Thought can be used in preparation as an entry slip, they can also be used as an "exit slip" that helps your students reflect on what they learned during the activity. Remember that for some students, writing will be their strongest voice and this is an opportunity for them to "speak" in that voice. The use of writing also supports students who need more time to organize their thoughts before sharing. The exit slips can be done on paper or digitally with the use of digital technology, allowing for the deadline to be extended beyond the final class bell. Some students will need this additional time to think and write. Giving those students different ways to share their thoughts beyond just what is said during the activity will give you more accurate insight into what the students are actually thinking and feeling and what they know about the topic.

Structured Academic Controversy

The biggest issue we have as social studies teachers is helping our students understand that there is no single superior perspective when studying societies, as social studies is a human-centered discipline. All humans are flawed and prone to biased thinking, so part of taking a disciplined approach is acknowledging our own biases and considering the stories about societies from multiple perspectives. We have to help the general population to understand that social studies inherently involves exploring events through multiple perspectives and point of views.

Luckily, we are witnessing an increased desire to want to know the whole story from all participants and bystanders. The structured academic controversy framework (Johnson & Johnson, 1988, 1993) allows students to delve into several points of view and communicate their findings in a predetermined format. The predetermined format gives students the experience to gain knowledge about the issues while gaining appreciation and respect for multiple viewpoints. Like many formats, the question is key. In the structured academic controversy (SAC) framework, students are to answer the question and come to consensus on the controversial issue. The consensus reinforces the idea that before students can choose a side, they need to consider all sides equally. Remember that the goal with a structured academic controversy is not to win; rather, SACs should give students adequate class time to present content knowledge and diverse perspectives as well as time for clarification questions, small-group discussion, large-group discussion, and consensus-building. Here are five steps for a SAC (adapted from Nathan & Lee, 2004):

1. **Learn and Prepare (10+ minutes):** Students are broken into groups. In their respective groups, students are provided information about the topic. They utilize this time as a group to find evidence to support the position they have been given. With more robust topics or readings, this preparation step may take an entire class period.
2. **Show and Tell (8–10 minutes per round):** Students present their perspective with evidence from what they have found. Each participant participates in the 3-minute time period. The other side is taking notes on what they hear and how the information that they have found challenges what may have been stated. After one side speaks, you may want to have the listening side summarize what they heard to ensure that the intended message was received. The roles of the two sides are then reserved, with the original listening side sharing their information and the original speaking side listening. Show and Tell may happen for one, two, or even three rounds as time allows.
3. **Talk and Think (10–15 minutes):** The students will engage in an open discussion, within a conversation. They are encouraged to assess the different positions based on the logic of the arguments and the extent of supporting evidence.
4. **Taking a New Approach (8–10 minutes):** In the same format as Show and Tell, students drop their original

perspective and pick up the opposite perspective. Students should try to include new points. This step is important as it helps students to understand the issue from different perspectives.

5. **Come Together (15–20 minutes):** Students come to a consensus and formulate an opinion on the topics based on the evidence from each perspective of the argument. The consensus is important because this will teach students the importance and value of collaborative conflict. During your first times using a SAC, it is important to define "consensus" with your students prior to asking them to reach a consensus.

After students have completed their SAC they are challenged to engage with the marginalized voices of the course and in the classroom. While SACs allow for students to enter into a variety of discourse roles and multiple perspectives, it is not the only strategy that we suggest to achieve those goals.

Inner and Outer Circle (or Fishbowl Discussion)

Every social studies teacher has an engaging question that will get the classroom really talking. In most situations, when the conversation is started there are a few students out of the class of 35 that have an opinion that is voiced. When tackling contentious conversations it is important for every voice to be given the opportunity to be heard. The inner-outer circle strategy is one of the best ways to have those conversations. We know there are several variations of this instructional strategy and any would be effective as long as all students equally participate in the conversation.

Setting the Stage

The question is important for this strategy as it encourages more student participation in discussion when they have a focus to share their thinking. We also suggest that students are made aware prior to class that they will be participating in the inner-outer circle discussion. There are several ways you can approach how the question or questions will be formulated (Table 5.2). As always, students should be provided with information to help them understand the topic so that there can be an informed discussion.

TABLE 5.2 Approaching Questions for Inner- and Outer-Circle Discussions

APPROACH	DESCRIPTION
Teacher centered	The teacher selects the topic and creates the main question and all guiding questions for the discussion. The teacher should be in the inner circle to keep the discussion going.
Student created	The teacher gives the students the topic. Students return to class with two to three questions each. In small groups they determine the one to two questions that will represent their group. The combined questions from the groups will be the questions for the discussion. Place the questions in a centralized place; when the discussion slows down, an outer-circle member gets a new question for the inner circle.
Mixed	The teacher and/or students help provide the focus of the topic and two to three guiding questions. Then students formulate questions they would like to hear before or during the class discussion. Add more questions as needed.

For the initial inner-outer circle, we suggest a teacher-centered approach with a noncontentious topic. Circle selection is important to ensure that all students get an opportunity to participate in the conversation. In most opportunities, we have seen that random selection of circle assignments with rotation is effective in showing that everyone has a speaking role. Each student chooses a card randomly from a bowl, basket, or box with an assigned role. There are two cards available: a discusser or an observer. The observer participates in the outer circle. The discusser participates in the inner circle. Each group, as well as the class in general, should be made aware of the role of the observer and discusser. It is often helpful to describe the roles on the cards that are selected.

- **Whole-Class Role (discussed prior):** Read or listen to all resources provided for the discussion. Be prepared to be chosen or selected in the inner or outer circle.
- **Discusser (inner circle):** These students will have an open discussion about today's important question.
- **Observer (outer circle):** These students' sole job is to listen to the conversation and take notes. There are several deviations of what this can look like:
    - *Notetaker*: Use two columns for notes. One column is the question that was asked and the other column is the response of the group.
    - *Convo Tracker*: The outer-circle member keeps track of questions, connections, inferences, evidence, and predictions. We normally assigned the outer-circle member two inner-circle members to watch. In this situation, multiple people should be watching specific inner-circle members.
    - *Phone a Friend*: The outer-circle member has strips of paper or sticky notes. The outer-circle member helps the inner-circle member with talking points by sliding them a strip of paper or note. Each outer-circle member only has two to three to use in a round.

At the end of the discussion, each student should complete a reflection activity. Some ideas include starting with a sentence stem ("At first, I thought . . . but now . . . ") or a 3-2-1 reflection (three points that were made, two connections or predictions I have, and one question I wish was asked). Requiring students to produce something at the end of the discussion helps students reflect on the main question and the topic.

Changing Up Inner-Outer Circle

The inner-outer circle can be differentiated to fit the class and students' skill set. Teachers can vary the strategy so it does not get boring for students.

1. **Provide Student Choice:** The inner circle can be a volunteer opportunity. You yield the opportunity to have more volunteers if students have been provided concise and efficient information on the topic. Remember the GUIDE process; if they know they have the answers, they are more willing to participate authentically. *Tip*: Require students to provide evidence showing that they read (e.g., marked-up text or sticky notes).
2. **Whose Seat Is It?** This variation of inner circle always gets students involved. Students take on the persona of influential individuals of the topic. Most would stick to individuals of the time period. We would suggest at least two not be individuals of the time period (i.e., at least one from prior to the event or topic and one current-day individual). We also suggest ensuring that diverse racial and gender roles are included as well. Students then read and research from the perspective of that individual. This work is done in advance and preferably in a group.
    a. Only students in the chairs can contribute to the discussion. The other group members are in the outer circle awaiting their opportunity to be in the chair.
    b. The person in the chair can contribute to the current discussion question or change the conversation. They can only bring up one issue and then leave. Each speaker cannot return to the chair until all their members have participated.

Socratic Seminar

Socratic Seminars are a good strategy for dialogue or discussion. The open-ended flow of this strategy does not work well for dividing students into pro/con groups and working toward determining a winner. There are four elements needed for an effective Socratic Seminar: a text, questions, seminar leader, and participants. Because of the text-dependent nature of this strategy, it is important to make sure that students have time to do a close read of the text in advance of the activity.

While the flow of discussion is more open ended than other strategies discussed in this chapter, the conversation should remain grounded in the text as much as possible. This is an opportunity to work on and reinforce critical skills related to stating a claim that is supported by evidence and explaining your reasoning in why the evidence supports that claim. When they are writing, students can clearly show connections between their evidence by using citations and quotes. These conversations should take place while the students have access to the texts that are being discussed. With these texts in hand, students can literally point to where they found the evidence that they are using to support their claim. If they cannot specifically point to a section of the text, then it is not allowed as evidence.

This can be taken up a level by having students "cite" where in the text they found the evidence as they speak, so that others in the class can follow along. An example would be, "In the last paragraph on page 27, they say . . ." It is worth noting that texts are not always written, and we encourage you to use not only narrative, written texts but also maps, charts, graphs, data sets, pictures, paintings, political cartoons, artifacts, music, videos, and more to support students when they are building background knowledge on a topic.

Once the text has been examined in preparation of the Socratic Seminar and procedures such as how evidence will be "cited" have been clearly laid out, it is time to begin the

Socratic Seminar. As best as possible, arrange students in a circle so that they can see each other. The seminar leader, traditionally the teacher to begin with, does not sit in the circle in an attempt to have students talk with each other as opposed to the seminar leader. Once the first question has been asked by the seminar leader, the floor is open for dialogue by the students. The role of the seminar leader is to keep the conversation on track, make sure that classroom agreements are followed, and when appropriate ask the next question to spark additional participant inquiry. The seminar leader should refrain from participating in the discussion and should only answer clarifying questions and correct or redirect participants in the procedures.

Students should focus on deep examination of the text through the questions posed by the seminar leader and the thoughts shared by other participants. There is not a goal of being "right" or finding the "right" answer. Students can be assessed by their ability to come up with questions for the group, the strength of their claims based on using evidence to develop clear reasoning, and how well the classroom agreements were followed. After the Socratic Seminar has ended, allow space and time for students to reflect on what they heard, especially aligned to the 3Cs of Thought and the development of their own thoughts along the way. Remember to allow for both verbal and written reflection when possible.

As your students become familiar with the structure of the Socratic Seminar, it is worth allowing students to take more of a lead in the facilitation of the seminar. The easiest way to do this is to have the students provide the questions that will be discussed. Since a Socratic Seminar works best with deep inquiry around open-ended questions, you can explore having students do the Question Formulation Technique (QFT) around the topic being discussed to develop questions that allow for the reflective thinking encouraged by a Socratic Seminar (Right Question Institute, 2021).

The QFT has students brainstorming (divergent thinking) about any and all questions that they could potentially think of related to the topic. Students then think about their questions to identify open-ended and closed-ended questions and make revisions as needed. With a list of questions in hand, students then work to narrow down the list (convergent thinking) of the "best" or "most important" questions to consider.

After the first reading of the text(s), have students work in small teams doing a QFT and submitting questions for consideration. Engaging in this process will help students take a bit of a different lens about the text(s) and help them take away new information as they read the text(s) a second time before the Socratic Seminar. With the addition of the QFT and a second reading, your students will be better equipped to participate in the conversation on the day of the Socratic Seminar. Scan the QR code to access the Right Question Institute website for more information on the QFT.

Scan the QR code to access the Right Question Institute website for more information on the Question Formulation Technique.

As students become adept at the structure of the Socratic Seminar and show the ability to ask questions that motivate thoughtful conversation, you may consider having students take the role of seminar leader. This can be done with an individual student or a small group of students, but the role remains the same as when the teacher was the seminar leader. The leader does not engage in the conversation directly; their role is to ask the questions and to make sure classroom agreements are followed.

Philosophical Chairs

Unlike Socratic Seminars, the Philosophical Chairs strategy is one that is set up to meet the goals related to a debate instead of a dialogue. The classroom should be set up with a section for "yes/support/pro" facing the section for "no/do not support/con," separated by an area for "undecided/do not know" and a space in the middle for the "hot seat." See Figure 5.1 as an example.

FIGURE 5.1 Philosophical Chairs

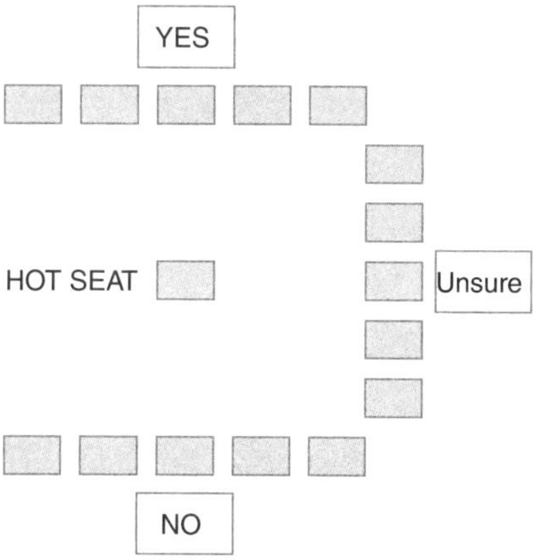

Again, there are different ways to group students for an activity like this. The most common approach is to give students the topic (either ahead of time or at the start of class) along with a question or stance about the topic and then ask students to arrange themselves by which section they would like to start in. A key component of Philosophical Chairs is that students are expected to move and that includes from one "side" to another as they see fit. Students should have already worked on developing background knowledge about the topic being discussed, but time may be needed for students to determine where they begin after hearing the question or statement that will be discussed or debated.

Once students have their starting spot, the teacher poses the question and then any side (including undecided) can take the spot in the hot seat in the middle of the room where they are given a time limit (usually starting at one minute) to speak about what they believe. At any point while someone is in the hot seat, students can "vote with their feet" by moving to a different section of the room. Movement does not mean that the student has necessarily changed their mind about the topic, but movement is encouraged to show real time "polling" about how the class views what is being said in the hot seat. Movement, while encouraged, does not mean that students are then expected to speak about why they switched positions, though oftentimes the switch is made so that they can speak in favor of or disagreement about what they just heard.

Once the speaker in the hot seat has finished, someone from a different section of the group is then allowed to take their spot and their one minute in the hot seat begins. It is important to note that students from the same section are not allowed to speak in succession unless the other two sections agree that nobody from their section is ready to speak. Also, once a student has spoken, that same student cannot speak until three turns have passed. Three turns would mean that someone from the other side, then someone from their side, and then someone else from the other side has had their turn to speak. This procedure is put in place to help ensure that one or two students do not dominate the discussion. You may modify procedures related to speaking time and how many turns must pass before a student can speak again based on the needs and personalities in your classroom for any given discussion. This is a great opportunity to get students involved in setting up agreements about how Philosophical Chairs will run in their classroom.

You may also consider adding in procedures such as having any student who speaks first summarizing what was said by the previous person. This encourages strong listening skills and clear communication. Also, since there is one clear hot seat speaker at a time, you may want to pair Philosophical Chairs with argument mapping to keep students engaged in the process of how the individual arguments all fit together. The addition of exit-slip reflection will help to keep all students engaged in the discussion, even when they are not in the hot seat.

You Be the Jury Adaptation of Philosophical Chairs

One adaptation of Philosophical Chairs is called You Be the Jury. Some students often select the "undecided/do not know" section because it is easy to keep saying "I don't know" as opposed to thinking deeply about the topic. In this adaptation, the setup is the same, but the focus is on the undecided students as they take turns in the hot seat and ask a question for consideration by the other two sections. Once the undecided student poses their question and leaves the hot seat, one student from "yes/pro" and one student from "no/con" each has their time in the hot seat. Like regular Philosophical Chairs, the two sides cannot use the same student for successive turns.

Once both sides complete their responses, the undecided student moves to either yes or no and explains why they believe that side gave the better answer. Stress to students that picking a side at this time does not mean that you believe completely in that side for the overall topic at hand, but rather that you believe that side made a more compelling argument related to your question. At this point, another student from the undecided section can ask their question from the hot seat and the process begins again until all undecided students have moved to a side. With any remaining time, the regular rules of Philosophical Chairs are back in play and students can move as they see fit.

Pinwheel Perspective-Taking

Pinwheel perspective-taking, adapted from Jennifer Gonzalez (2015) of Cult of Pedagogy, is a strategy to encourage multiple points of view and reasoning in a more structured protocol. The class is broken into four (or more depending on class size) different groups. One group is assigned the role of "provocateur," while the other groups are all assigned a different perspective that they will represent. Challenge yourself and your students to think beyond the idea of "yes, I support this idea" and "no, I am against this idea" to search for more precise reasoning and evidence about why they support one side. When it comes to contentious topics, even if you can boil it down to yes or no, inside each of those two sides there will be varying perspectives about why the answer is yes or no.

For instance, let's consider the question, "Should the United States raise the minimum wage to $15 an hour?" Some of those saying yes might focus on the fact that the federal minimum wage has not been raised since 2009 and has not kept up with inflation; therefore, many people who work full-time, minimum-wage jobs are living below the poverty line. Another yes perspective might focus on gender issues, as women are more likely than men to have a job that pays minimum wage. Those saying no might think about how increasing wages would increase the costs of production and raise the costs of products and therefore not actually help people purchase more. Another no perspective could address that this should be a local issue, since the cost of living varies significantly from place to place.

Pinwheel perspective-taking puts students into a position of taking a stance on an issue that is narrow enough to help them focus when researching. It also helps to make sure that the class hears from and learns about a wider array of perspectives than if the students only focused on the perspectives that they would have originally brought to the table. The role of the provocateur is to then ask questions of the students with different perspectives and engage in conversation with them so that those different perspectives can be shared and thought about more in depth.

Within the groups, procedures can be put into place (1) to establish how the students determine who will speak for their group and how long they will speak and (2) to provide clarity around how the group rotates and works together to make sure that all group members are involved. Depending on the experience of the group, questions can be prepared and presented ahead of time (again think of using the QFT) or the perspective groups can be doing their research while the provocateur group is writing appropriate questions for the perspective groups to answer during the activity. Teachers can also consider having students determine which perspectives need to be included in the activity. Before starting down the path of doing their research or taking a stance, students could pitch or propose who and why should be included based on background knowledge or initial information shared with the class. This would make a strong connection to the T (Talk) component of the LETS ACT Framework discussed in Chapter 4.

Gallery Walks

Gallery walks are a way to have students engage with a contentious topic in a written format. Gallery walks can be set up in a variety of different ways to best align with the goals that you have for your students for this task. Things to consider when setting up your gallery walk include what texts and perspectives will be presented, what question(s) students will respond to, and how their responses will be recorded.

The most straightforward gallery walk includes texts that were preselected by the teacher for student consideration. Be sure to consider visual-based texts, like maps, charts, graphs, pictures, and so on, as a way to support students of different reading levels and promote data literacy. Longer or more difficult readings can pose problems for students who need time to reread or process. These texts are spaced out around the room so that students have space to gather around each of the texts in small groups for the determined amount of time before rotating to the next text.

During their time with a text, students should be responding to either an overarching question that relates to all of the texts, a question that is specific to the text that they are currently working with, or both. When possible, have an overarching compelling question that ties all of the texts together, but include an additional question or two with each text to help students focus and think more deeply about that specific text. Have the goal be that students are able to make connections within the individual texts while also seeing the bigger picture of different ways that the texts can potentially fit together in support of their answer to the overarching question. When students are working with each text, give them clear directions about how they should be recording their thoughts. Graphic organizers can be provided to help students better compose their thoughts, especially as they relate to an overarching question that may require them to pull evidence or thoughts from multiple texts while composing a final response.

One additional option for capturing student responses is to put chart paper up in each station and have students record their thoughts for others to see. This can be done by students individually or as a statement that reflects a consensus of the group. After the first rotation, students can be instructed to either respond to the original question as the first group did or to respond to the thoughts of the first group. This can continue with each rotation so that students are sharing new thoughts about the question, responding to a previous comment with a different idea, or building off a previous comment to expand their own thinking. This version of a gallery walk starts to blend the qualities of students interacting with each other like in a classroom discussion or debate, while helping to focus the conversation on the associated text. The time needed to read and write responses also slows down the speed and emotions of what is being said and makes it less likely for a student to say something they might regret. If students are responding as individuals, then there is potential for inappropriate comments to be provided without being able to track them back to a specific individual—so plan accordingly when it comes to how groups work together while at their station.

WHAT IF IT GOES WRONG?

Laying the foundation from the first four chapters of this book should get you as close as possible to *not* have anything go wrong. That being said, there is no way to make anything in your classroom 100% error-proof and this is true for contentious conversations. Both of us have had experiences in the classroom where in spite of our best efforts, there were still students who were upset or parents called or emailed with concerns or a complaint. As school-, district-, and state-level education leaders, we both have had experiences where we have had to support educators or districts where issues have arisen. So as much as we would like to tell you that you won't have any issues, this section is your reminder to lean on the supports that you have put in place for when things do go wrong.

The 3Ps (policies, protocols, and procedures) are like an insurance policy for your classroom. You do not want to be in a situation to use them, but you will be happy you have them when the time comes. Ask yourself the following:

- Is your administration aware of your 3Ps and is there a clear plan for them to support you?

- Are your students' parents aware of your 3Ps and have you given them advance notice about what will happen if a student does not follow the 3Ps?
- Do you have a clear plan for handling an individual student that says something inappropriate or does not follow classroom agreements?
- Can you clearly articulate the skills that are being worked on in each activity and describe why the chosen topic fits into both your curriculum and the skill development?
- Are you using a classroom strategy that is set up with clear rules, expectations, and intended outcomes?

Being able to answer all of these questions does not mean that students and family members will not be upset, but it does give you and your administrators a clear ground to stand on. Remember that your curriculum is district/state approved and never lose sight of the pedagogical reasons for doing what you did in the classroom. Planning ahead is intended to keep you from reacting in a way that makes a bad situation worse. You created a plan for a reason. Stick to your plan and keep your administration involved as much as possible.

Restorative Circles

Even after navigating any issues with the student directly or with concerned family or community members, there will still be a need to address how what happened impacted the other students in the classroom. We recommend using restorative circles in your classroom after any situation that "goes wrong." Not only does the research show success in the use of restorative circles (Fronius et al., 2019; van Woerkom, 2018), but if you have created a plan as outlined in this book, then you are already set up to implement restorative circles in your classroom.

Restorative circles start with having a safe, supportive space that is built before the first day of class. All of the work invested in day-zero and day-one planning sets the stage for the safe space not only for the contentious conversations but also for the restorative circles if needed. As the facilitator, you need to be prepared for the emotion that may come out when students reflect on how they feel about what happened in your class. Anticipating the needs of the group and planning ahead will help to make sure that students feel that they are in a safe space to share. While you were using Chapters 2 and 3 to set up your contentious topics, you were also aligning your practice with the idea of preparing and planning ahead. A restorative circle will need the same attention to detail that you already know is important in supporting your students.

When it comes time to have your students participate in the restorative circle, the same classroom culture that you developed to talk about contentious topics will be utilized for this discussion as well. Students will need to be invited into a conversation where they feel safe and that they are being heard. To help focus on one speaker at a time, many restorative circles use a *talking piece* to symbolize the only person who should be speaking at that time. A talking piece can be just about any physical object, but we recommend that the talking piece only be brought out during a restorative circle in order to emphasize the importance of the conversation and the role that the talking piece plays in that conversation.

Like during a contentious conversation, having students paraphrase each other while acknowledging that everyone is bringing different backgrounds and experiences to this conversation is crucial. Students who have been hurt by what happened will need to feel empathy from others in the class. In the best-case scenario, this would include an apology and empathy from the student(s) who was at the heart of the "when it goes wrong" situation, but that might not always be possible. Work to make sure that students understand how they can be an ally to those who were hurt even if they were not the one who caused the pain. Talking about shared experiences may be a difficult but important part of the healing.

A restorative circle is also an opportunity to explore not just the individuals involved in what happened but also how this represents issues that are bigger than the classroom. Students may want to talk about how "what went wrong" impacts students who are not in the room as well as individuals in society as a whole. Just like a discussion about a contentious topic blends individual students' perspectives with a larger view of society, the same can be done with a restorative circle. It is highly likely that what happened in your classroom is not an isolated, unique event and students may need to make connections about how "what went wrong" is reflective of a world that is bigger than the classroom.

Just like how having a plan will not prevent issues from arising, having a restorative circle will most likely not heal all wounds completely and immediately. That does not mean that time should not be taken to start the healing process. Structures and a plan were needed to help students have contentious conversations and structures and plans will be needed if something goes wrong. While we acknowledge that things may go wrong and ask that you plan ahead for that, we also urge you to not let this possibility scare you away from addressing these topics. While there is potential for having issues arise in your classroom, with proper planning and support, your classroom is the safest place for students to talk about the issues that our society struggles with every day. Your students need you even when it does not always go according to plan.

CLOSING REFLECTION

- What do we want students to learn from the contentious topic conversation?
- How will you work to ensure that every voice is heard in the discussion?
- What do you have in place for reflection for both yourself and your students?
- Why is it important to have a clear plan of action for when "things go wrong"? How will this be communicated to students, parents, and your administration?

Now that you have read this chapter, you should be able to complete the following:

- ✓ Design your classroom to support successful student participation in civil discourse.
- ✓ Identify strategies that you will implement in your classroom when discussing contentious topics.
- ✓ Determine which contentious topics of your curriculum best align with each of those strategies.
- ✓ Identify what strategies will work best with your students based on grade level.
- ✓ Make a plan for how you will handle when something goes wrong while students are engaging in discourse.

CHAPTER 6

Growth

Improving and Expanding Our Impact

While the search for answers and the struggle to implement them is indeed difficult and time-consuming, the real methodology for system change begins and ends with ongoing, authentic conversations about the important questions.

—Tony Wagner (1993)

This chapter will help to prepare you to complete the following:

- ✓ Advocate for a curriculum that supports civil discourse.
- ✓ Familiarize yourself with a pedagogical triangle that supports curriculum review and revisions.
- ✓ Determine the current status of a current or upcoming curriculum review in your district and identify areas of strengths and weakness.

(Continued)

(Continued)

- ✓ Do a SWOT (Strengths, Weaknesses, Opportunities, Threats) analysis of current curriculum to identify where civil discourse skills can be added or improved.
- ✓ Seek out and support colleagues who can serve as an ally in amplifying your work.
- ✓ Engage in reflective practice about your classroom and curriculum.

Up to this point, the focus of this book has been on building toward the day in class when students will engage in a conversation about the most contentious topics. *How do I do this?* is the question that we hear the most and inspired us to write this book, but real change in our educational systems needs more than pockets of excellence. Looking to help build a community that comes together to strengthen all members means that students will need consistent and ongoing support in working with each other to discuss the biggest issues our society struggles with. In this chapter, we look at how you will make a bigger impact beyond a couple of days of great learning in your classroom.

Take a moment and reflect on the following questions:

- What are your "go-to" teaching moves to get students engaged in their learning?
- Think about your favorite teacher(s) that you have had. What did they do to get you engaged in your learning?
- Where in your current curriculum is there space for students to engage in conversations about "divergent opinions"?
- Are there educators in your building, district, or professional learning network whose work you admire?

How did you become aware of their work and how can you work to bring others into contact with them as professionals?

- How do you search for professional development opportunities to grow as an educator? Do you believe that you have access to enough ongoing training and support?

A BIG-PICTURE APPROACH

The contentious topics teachers choose to discuss do not have to be hot-button issues of today for students to practice their skills of discourse. If historians are not able to reach consensus on many parts of United States history, then we should not expect our students to do so either.

> To historians, history is an argument about what facts should or shouldn't mean. Even when historians are able to piece together the basic story of what happened, they rarely agree about what an event means or what caused it. Historians argue about the past's meaning and what it has to tell us in the present. (Wineburg, 2010, p. 2)

While more than 50% of our youngest voters voted in the 2020 election (CIRCLE, 2020, 2021), young voters still have the lowest voter turnout by age group. If one of the goals of our educational system is to prepare our students to be civically engaged, then we must engage them in learning about civic participation. Teachers report hesitation in feeling comfortable and supported in their ability to teach about elections in the social studies classroom. Multiple data points tell us that educators are feeling concerns ranging from a lack of administrative support to fears of community and parent pushback (Humphries, 2020; Southern Poverty Law Center, 2016).

One of the more fundamental topics in many of our social studies classrooms is now considered contentious: elections (Williams, 2021). If we are not going to teach about elections in our social studies classrooms, then where are students supposed to get the basic knowledge necessary to participate in them? While we understand the potentially contentious nature of different parts of our content, it is still our job to develop and deliver a curriculum that meets the needs of our students. As described in a Visions of Education (2020) podcast, Dr. Dan Krutka, Associate Professor of Social Studies Education at North Texas University, implores his preservice educators to think about this question: "When you are fearful of teaching a topic, who are you thinking about?" We must not allow students to miss out on critical learning due to our own personal fears, just like we know that we must not allow our own personal beliefs to impact the teaching of the curriculum.

Student involvement in discussion also extends beyond voter engagement. Dr. Kei Kawashima-Ginsberg (2013), Director of the Tufts University Center for Information and Research on Civic Learning and Engagement (CIRCLE), examined 2010 National Assessment of Educational Progress (NAEP) data. Kawashima-Ginsberg found that high school students who engaged in debates and interactive discussions more than once a month scored higher on the NAEP than their counterparts who engaged in debates and interactive discussions less than once a month. Discourse led to higher NAEP scores regardless of race, gender, or socioeconomic status.

The NAEP data show a positive impact for both eighth-grade and high school students who engaged in discussions about current events at least weekly. Why do we see this level of impact when students engage in discussions around the type of topics that we often avoid in our classrooms? According to Van Benthuysen and Hodgin (2019), Dr. Diana Hess and Dr. Paula McAvoy found that "when students engaged in high-quality discussion they enjoyed their classes more, were interested in what their peers had to say, deepened their understanding of issues, and . . . didn't demonize difference!"

This impact is not specifically about the topics themselves, but rather the approach in which the topics are handled. There is not a list of specific questions that can be added to a curriculum in order to build this type of student engagement. What is required is buy-in from both curriculum developers and educators to allow students to explore the gray areas of both our historical and contemporary world through their own lens. When we understand that the way we see the world is unique for each of us and each of our students, then that frees us to step back from what we as educators believe is true and allow for our students to expand their own beliefs through interactions with others.

MAKING CONNECTIONS

Districts looking to revise curriculum in a manner that supports contentious conversations are usually looking for a specific step-by-step approach. This can be especially difficult when the curricular review is also seeking to ensure that justice, equity, diversity, and inclusion are prevalent and appropriately covered as part of a district's curriculum. While there are processes in place for districts to review and revise their curricula, these revisions have been repeated for decades without really getting to the heart of the role that curriculum plays in how we view ourselves and those around us. If we do what we have always done, then we will get what we have always gotten. To make lasting and impactful change, the work has to be approached from a different angle.

Contentious topics are key to having the type of conversations that we avoided for decades in our classrooms and for centuries in our society. It is the contentious nature of many of these topics that led many textbook publishers and districts themselves to produce curricula that use a noncontentious lens in presenting information. The approach of centering the stories of certain groups while avoiding the many uncomfortable truths of history brings us to the current day where we now have tension around how curriculum should be developed (American Historical Association, 2021). We must understand that a balanced approach to the social studies curriculum is what will make our communities stronger.

Discussing contentious issues as described in this book provides more opportunities to celebrate the historical diversity of our country by addressing issues of justice and equity instead of turning away from them, while working to ensure that teachers are focused on students engaging with the appropriately approved curriculum. As author Robert Jones Jr. (2015) says, "We can disagree and still love each other unless your disagreement is rooted in my oppression and denial of my humanity and right to exist." While we want to make sure that students are versed in the skills that lead to civil discourse, we must make sure that the content in which they are practicing those skills is not set upon the same foundation as previous iterations while honoring the experiences that our students bring to the classroom.

Any shift in thinking means those in power have to understand their role in the development and perpetuation of the current system and then be willing to lead the work to change the system. When the shift involves addressing a long history of oppression and discrimination or changing our classroom approach, not everyone will be ready to make the shift at the same time. Many will not be ready to even engage in those conversations, which means that the discussions will most likely be contentious. In her Netflix special *The Call to Courage*, Brené Brown reminds us, "We have to be able to choose courage over comfort . . . Brave leaders are never silent around hard things. Our job is to excavate the unsaid" (Restrepo, 2019). The ability of all school leaders to be able to participate in these discussions is necessary to create and implement a quality curriculum.

The adults in the schools are not the only ones who may struggle when a curriculum changes in its approach. The impact will be felt beyond our school walls as parents and community members will face a curriculum that is different from what they know. This change will move them out of their comfort zones and may lead to resistance, which must be planned for as part of the curricular review. Take time to listen to as many voices in your community as you can and, when possible, include competing views in your curriculum development. Work to get everyone on the same page about the *why* and the *how* of the work so they can help others understand the work and help keep people from being caught off guard.

Once the foundation is in place, the question of where to begin implementing change comes next. Just as we want to engage students in conversations without a specific correct answer in mind, leaders must also know that there is not always one answer. Those leading the work should not think of this as a linear progression, as the work itself has to be pursued in a way that makes the most sense for each district. This means there may be multiple ways to start the work and many options for how the work connects and evolves. Facing History and Ourselves (2021a) has a pedagogical triangle for historical and civic understanding, which gives us three main entry points and makes connections among each of these entry points. More importantly, the use of the pedagogical triangle reminds us that unlike linear progressions, one can begin a triangle at any point and there is no true end point to the work.

Facing History and Ourselves (2021a) describes each part of the pedagogical triangle as follows: "The arrows between intellectual rigor, emotional engagement, and ethical reflection are bidirectional, as these processes strengthen each other. At the center is students' civic agency, their belief that they can play a positive role in their peer groups, schools, communities, and the larger world." How does this connect to discussions about contentious topics? The pedagogical triangle can be used "to foster students' historical understanding, critical thinking, and empathy and other social–emotional learning competencies, and *facilitate transformative dialogue in their classrooms* [emphasis added]" (Facing History and Ourselves, 2021a). What role does the pedagogical triangle play in facilitating transformative dialogue?

Inspired by the Facing History and Ourselves pedagogical triangle, we created our own version shown in Figure 6.1. We use language that is a bit more teacher friendly and common in everyday practice in schools. Intellectual rigor is replaced by and is met with rigorous, appropriate, and *high-quality content* for classroom use. Ethical reflection is replaced by and is met with *curriculum review and revision*. Emotional engagement is replaced by and is met with *self-, student, and staff reflection*. These changes were made in response to educators asking for the "right" materials and lessons to teach certain subject areas. However, we do not believe that simply inserting a certain unit brings the impact that we are looking for. Students need to make connections beyond content.

The pedagogical triangle allows us to move beyond the idea that just introducing certain pieces of content into the classroom curriculum will lead to "transformative dialogue." For example, social studies textbooks (especially history textbooks) for years have ensured that "Famous Women in History" shows up in a little text box on the bottom of page 27 and "Famous African Americans in History" shows up in a separate text box at the top of page 43. Without the appropriate context, support, or discussion, this content does little to facilitate critical thinking. While representation is important, it is what is done with that information that is essential

FIGURE 6.1 Our Pedagogical Triangle

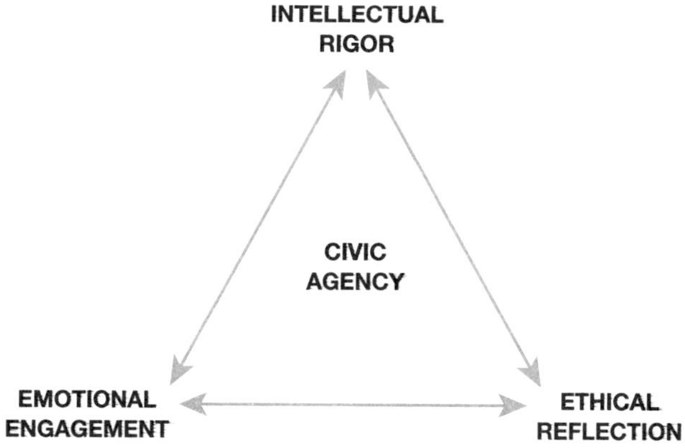

SOURCE: Adapted from Facing History and Ourselves (2021a).

to student learning. Developing a depth of understanding necessary to see the multiple perspectives inherent in our history and the contentious topics of today is more than inserting a text box about an underrepresented group or hot-button topic of the moment.

Background knowledge is only the beginning of student learning. Dr. Norman Webb identified the four levels of depth of knowledge and students must be pushed across all four in order to "truly engage in deep learning over time" (Albuquerque Public Schools, n.d.; Walsh & Sattes, 2016). While the "intellectual rigor" of the content is a key component of student learning, it is not the only piece, nor does it have to be the starting place. The integration of content can happen after what Facing History and Ourselves (2021a) calls an "ethical reflection," which we connect to while doing a curriculum review. This review is required for successful implementation of updated content that better aligns with the belief that we will encourage students to engage in discussions around contentious topics. Content that is not coordinated as part of a larger sense of purpose in the curriculum has little impact on student learning, just as a curriculum review that does not yield any updated content lacks the potential to shift how students learn.

The third side of the pedagogical triangle for historical and civic understanding is what Facing History and Ourselves (2021a) calls "emotional engagement" and we connected to self-, student, and staff reflection. This is the work that we all have to do as individuals and with our peers to understand our own thoughts and emotions. Getting ourselves, fellow staff, and our students involved in examining our internal emotional engagement means that we are able to properly deliver the curriculum as intended. This means that we teach in a manner that is aligned with social–emotional learning competencies that helps to ensure we are not artificially introducing barriers to student learning.

The most well-thought-out, research-based curriculum will still fall flat if the educators delivering the curriculum are not aware of the way that they impact student learning. This can be done both intentionally and unintentionally through our words and actions, but impactful just the same. Just as we want students to be self-reflective learners, we need to ensure that we are self-reflective practitioners who are equipped to deliver quality instruction for our students.

Once all three sides of the pedagogical triangle are examined, then classrooms can be places for active engagement in civil discourse. Topics that our society deems contentious, both past and present, should be at the forefront of student learning in order to produce students who participate in our democratic republic through civic engagement. Civic engagement is necessary to have the conversations required to develop and implement the ideas that will shape our future. As educators, our job is to develop and deliver rigorous content created through intense ethical reflection and to deliver it with an understanding of the emotional engagement of both our educators and our students. Only then can we make good on the promise of education that prepares the next generation of citizens.

EXPANDING YOUR IMPACT

Developing civic engagement is not something that we can do alone in our society nor can we do it alone in our schools. Having individual educators engaging in high-quality civil discourse about contentious topics is a great start, but pockets of excellence are not enough. To make meaningful and long-lasting change, we need a big-picture approach that supports both our students and educators. There needs to be a vision that is supported by both educators and administrators to work on all three sides of the pedagogical triangle for historical and civic understanding. These are the required first steps in making the systematic changes necessary for this essential work to take root, and you will need allies.

Look around your building and district and identify who is already doing the work and who can support the work that you want to do. Start small and reach out to educators that you admire. What do they do that you want to do better? Once you have identified the helpful learning that these teachers are able to share, then make sure to spread the word to others. The goal is not to give these strong educators more work to do, but rather to help people recognize the strengths that many of us already have. If your school has scheduled time for professional learning communities (PLCs) or regular department meetings, ask for time to be put on the agenda to share and ask questions about what others are doing in their classroom when nobody else is watching. What is it that they do to get students engaged, have successful conversations, and build community?

Educators tend to be humble heroes. If you ask most educators to share what they do best, many of them will initially respond by not knowing or being able to think of anything. We have observed hundreds, if not thousands, of teachers in the course of our work. From each observation, we always take away at least one thing that we would like to share with other educators—good ideas, best practices, or quality examples of how to teach better. When we point this out to educators, they often do not see it as anything special but rather just "something they do" in the classroom. Pockets of excellence are great, but they do not make for sustainable learning for students. Help your peers spread their excellence by promoting them to others and celebrating the great things that they do.

By fostering a collaborative culture in which current best practices are celebrated, moving the work forward becomes more about building a foundation that supports what is already working for you and your peers. Too often, the idea of change is overwhelming because it is presented as all the things that need to change based on what is going wrong. Instead, approach the work as this: we are 98% of the way there and these are the changes that will push us to the top. This approach will help with the buy-in for those who will actually do the implementation of the identified changes in their classrooms. Success will be at least partially defined by the frequency and consistency in which students are exposed to the quality curriculum that you are seeking.

Once you have identified who excels in the work that you want to achieve, start looking to turn them into allies. Unless you are an administrator in a key position, it is unlikely that your motivation to do this work will be enough to make significant change, so you will need additional support. In order to keep the work manageable, keep your first goals small. We suggest that you try to get buy-in from about 20% of the impacted group. This might be your grade level, your department, or your building, depending on how far reaching your work is.

The group of 20% is enough of a critical mass to approach your administration about looking to make systemic, long-term change. Identify what it is you hope to do, the steps necessary to do so, and how you will get additional staff on board and involved. The work that is most directly addressed in this book will most likely be a combination of curriculum development and professional development for staff, but it is possible to focus on any parts of the pedagogical triangle identified earlier in this chapter as your starting place. If they are not already involved, this is the time to bring your department chairs and curriculum coordinators into the work. They will be critical in framing the big picture and developing the supports to make the work sustainable in the long term.

We believe that shifts in curriculum will bring the most initial success because curriculum supports the development of the skills identified in Chapter 4 in a way that is necessary for effective learning of critical knowledge and skills. Students will not be successful with their first couple attempts nor should students stop practicing the skills of deliberation and disagreement once they achieve success. Developing the ability to engage in civil discourse will be an ongoing process throughout their life.

Another reason we focus on building quality curriculum to support student deliberation is to address a fear that many educators have when students talk about contentious issues: keeping teachers and schools out of the news! As Julie Underwood (2017), a noted scholar on educational law, tells us:

> Teachers face particular challenges when they are teaching political or controversial topics in classrooms. They must navigate a narrow passage between delivering the curriculum as required by their local board of education and sharing their own personal views and other information, while also

> abiding by board regulations regarding content and delivery. In addition, they must deliver the curriculum without attempting to indoctrinate students with their own personal beliefs, particularly on religious, political, and controversial topics.

So while we remind educators that they must play in the sandbox of the curriculum that they are given, school districts can support their educators by giving them a sandbox worth playing in.

The list of potential topics is too broad and the spectrum of district courses is too wide for us to even begin to consider offering up specific ideas for inclusion in your curriculum. However, whatever topics your district chooses to include or not include, we suggest that some of the following ideas and concepts are included in a broad sense:

- Students will engage in the three deliberative activities of discourse (dialogue, discussion, and debate).
- Historical and contemporary events will be examined for similarities and differences as well as potential cause and effect.
- Speaking and listening skills will be identified and evaluated as part of classroom activities.
- Students will be allowed to take a stance on the topic of their choosing and be evaluated based on state and district writing standards.
- Claims, evidence, and reasoning will be the focus of argumentative writing and students will be required to address counterclaims of their position.
- Media literacy and informational literacy will be highlighted as students cite evidence and determine reliability of their findings.

With a plan in place and administrative support, the goal of the 20% is to build your coalition of the willing (Table 6.1). Your "early adopters" believed in the idea from the beginning, but many of your peers will need to be convinced. This is the 60–70% of staff that when added to your first 20% becomes the "critical mass" and driving force for the work. A combination of administrative leadership, department/school planning time, curriculum review, and professional development will be needed to explain the *why* and *how* of the work to this 60–70%. They want what is best for students and staff, but they need to see and understand the plan before

TABLE 6.1 Working With Colleagues

WHO THEY ARE	WHAT THEY DO	MAKEUP OF STAFF
Early adopters	This is you and your allies that will lead the work. With administrative support, this group develops a plan.	20%
Critical mass	This group willingly participates in professional development and thoughtfully contributes to the idea. When presented with the *why* and *how*, they can be brought on board to support the work. However, this group will eventually lose interest and/or withdraw support if incremental progress is not made.	60–70%
Naysayers	This group is not interested in change. They have seen too many "fads" come and go and/or believe what they are doing is already the best path forward. It can be too difficult and time consuming to get them on board.	10–20%

jumping in. While they might not be on board from the beginning, they are your critical mass necessary to do the work. They will take some time, but if you have a good plan, allies, and administrative support, they can and will be convinced.

It is important for us to note that in almost every curriculum review and professional learning environment we have ever encountered, there are always naysayers. Know this from the beginning and do not allow them to distract you from the goal. This last 10–20% of staff and peers will always be there no matter how you approach the work. Our experience tells us that the biggest threat they pose to your work is not that they will never get on board. The issue with the naysayers is that when your focus is trying to convince them and getting to 100% buy-in and support, the time and energy spent on them eventually takes away from the time and energy spent on the 60–70% critical mass. In time, they may leave your cause.

Reflect on projects and initiatives that you have participated in during your professional experience.

- Was there at least one member of the group that was never happy about the work or satisfied with the direction or vision?
- Were you ever in the 60–70% critical mass, and did you get frustrated that the trainings or meetings seemed to be talking about the same things over and over again?
- How much of this was in an attempt to "get everyone on board" even though most of the group was already on board?
- Did you eventually lose interest in the work because instead of taking next steps, the work was continually reviewed in an attempt to appease or convince the naysayer?

Most of the educators that we talk to about this have had experiences like we describe. Do not fall for the trap of trying to get 100% agreement, as this will most likely be the leading reason why the work fails. Just like we would never expect every student in our classroom to share a belief, we cannot believe that every educator will come to the same agreement and understanding. Instead think about the ideas from this book that were framed for classroom conversations. Instead focus on how much of the group needs to be on board (pick less than 100%). When you are identifying next steps, think about how the naysayers will be addressed in spite of the continuation of the work. Your administration will be key in helping to navigate the work when 80% of a department wants to make a curriculum change but 20% is resistant. The 20% should be heard but should not allow the work to stop completely. Focus on keeping your coalition of 80% motivated to continue the work and that is where you will find success.

REFLECTING TO IMPROVE

> Reflective practice is "learning through and from experience towards gaining new insights of self and practice."
>
> Linda Finlay (2008)

Reflective practice is a means by which we look to tomorrow by first looking at what we have already experienced. In this case, each experience of conversations and deliberation in the classroom is a point that gives us feedback that will inform our tomorrow. There is no magic formula for ensuring that your students always succeed in having conversations about contentious topics. Nor is there a smooth timeline of steps that need to be followed. In reality, each set of students from year to year and from hour to hour will have unique strengths and pose different challenges.

These challenges are opportunities for growth with our students if we view them as such and take time to reflect on a work in progress. There are many who worry if people, our students included, are capable of engaging in civil discourse in an era where so much about how we communicate seems broken. As educators, our job is to teach our students how to communicate with each other and to view this skill as a constant work in progress as opposed to one that is broken and beyond repair. The mistakes that our students make, and they will make mistakes, will be presented to you to help understand what works and what needs to be worked on.

How do you reflect on both the good and the not so good in your classroom? F. M. Quinn (1998) examined different models for reflection and found that most tend to use three steps:

1. Retrospection
2. Self-evaluation
3. Reorientation

As mentioned in Chapter 3, students should be engaging in this process when it comes to the classroom agreements. You can help students better understand this process by modeling these three steps in your own work. Make it clear with your students that you will be checking in on them regarding how activities related to contentious topics went. The check-in does not mean that they did anything wrong; rather, it is part of your reflective practice. By checking in, you are getting a sense of where they are at, what they need, and what can be done to meet those needs in your classroom.

Whether you are engaging in classroom activities about contentious topics for the first time or making changes to how you approach the work, make a plan for how you will capture your thoughts and the thoughts of your students. For your students, this can be a quick exit-slip narrative or a questionnaire with a 1–5 Likert scale to capture feedback. A combination of the two will allow you to have both data points in your work as well as specific thoughts from your students. We are not suggesting that this should be done every day; rather, look at the activities that focus on the skill-building identified in Chapter 4 to help build your progress map.

Before you look at the student feedback, write down your own reflections about what you thought went well and what did not go well and then rate (on a 1–5 scale) both how you think the students did in their role and how you did in your role. Doing this before seeing what the students wrote and how they rated the day will help make sure that your reflections are not influenced by the students. A couple times a year, especially during your most contentious topic activities, you may also want to consider bringing in a peer, mentor, or administrator to give another perspective on how things went. While it is understandable to worry about things going wrong and having an administrator there, the opportunity for them to see your protocols, policies, and procedures in action is invaluable for everyone.

With this feedback in hand, it is time to dig into how the activity unfolded the way that it did. Are there any common themes that emerge as you are looking through the students' thoughts? If so, are those themes (both positive and negative) ones that were in your control or were there factors going on outside of your classroom that impacted how the activity was perceived? When you are working with contentious topics, especially ones that are talked about by the community, news, and social media, there may be unavoidable spillover into your classroom.

For the feedback that is related to things in your control, this is the time to examine what needs to stay and what needs to change. Positive outcomes should be built upon and reinforced moving forward. Outcomes that missed that mark need to be addressed and potentially redone in your classroom. There is no way to rush students when it comes to being prepared and skilled in deliberative activities. Much like a spelling or math test, students should be able to use the basic foundational skills essential to the activity. If they cannot, then this must be addressed before moving on to the next activity; otherwise, the same issues are likely to arise.

Deciding whether or not to move forward or to try again is your reorientation reflection. The curriculum and lesson plans are developed with the plan of successful implementation. In the classroom, educators know that this is rarely the case. It is through reflective practice that educators paint on the canvas that is their classroom each and every day. Some days it is more of one thing and less of something else. This is part of the reason why we have already put an emphasis on curriculum reviews. The review of an entire curriculum or the reflection on your classroom should be viewed as an opportunity to better align to the needs of your students, the resources available, and your own skills as an educator.

The reorientation is partly about what is going on in your classroom, but it is also partly about your skills as an educator who wants to facilitate deliberations about contentious topics in your classroom. Just as you will check in with your students about their skills related to these conversations, it is essential that you do the same as an educator. Continually checking in through the year gives you a way to reflect on your curriculum, lesson plans, and best practices once the year is complete.

Work with your PLC, grade level, or content area teams or even your school and district to develop a professional learning plan that includes growth related to supporting contentious topics in your classroom. Have you met the goals that you set for yourself when you started to learn more? What are your new goals for the upcoming school year? Seek out professional development opportunities that align to areas of need that you have identified. Do not forget that this learning may be found by your colleague right down the hall.

Are you looking to expand your learning beyond the walls of your school, but budget constraints limit what can be paid for? Check out the QR code for a list of trainings and resources that you may find helpful in meeting your goals as a professional.

Scan the QR code for a list of trainings and resources that you may find helpful in meeting your goals as a professional educator.

CLOSING REFLECTION

- Where will you begin to support the use of civil discourse around contentious topics in your classroom and in your district?
- Who are the agents of change in your school or district? How do you become involved in the work that they are doing in order to bring your voice to the table?
- Who do you see as your "allies" in this work? Who are your potential "naysayers"?
- What are the *whys* that will build your coalition in supporting the work?
- How do you currently collect feedback on your work? Do you see all three levels of reflection? Where do you anticipate areas to add or adapt how you reflect moving forward?

Now that you have read this chapter, you should be able to complete the following:

- ✓ Advocate for a curriculum that supports civil discourse.
- ✓ Familiarize yourself with a pedagogical triangle that supports curriculum review and revisions.
- ✓ Determine the current status of a current or upcoming curriculum review in your district and identify areas of strengths and weakness.
- ✓ Do a SWOT (Strengths, Weaknesses, Opportunities, Threats) analysis of current curriculum to identify where civil discourse skills can be added or improved.
- ✓ Seek out and support colleagues who can serve as an ally in amplifying your work.
- ✓ Engage in reflective practice about your classroom and curriculum.

Conclusion

Staying the Course and Continuous Improvement

> *A journey of a thousand miles begins with a single step.*
>
> —Lao Tzu

Congratulations! You have taken at least one step in your journey to supporting students and working with other educators when it comes to having conversations about contentious topics. These conversations may be related to hot-button political issues or light-hearted topics that have people laughing their way through the disagreement. The work may need to focus on scope and sequences across a district as well as lesson plans in your classroom. Your first step may be as simple as using the term *contentious* instead of *controversial.* Whatever you see as the first takeaway to be implemented, you have started down the path of this necessary work.

Changes to curriculum and classroom practice will not happen overnight and require support. This book describes the CUBED framework—Courage to embrace our discomfort and come together as a group; Understanding of key terms, ideas, and goals; Belonging for all, including differing thoughts, views, culture and abilities; Empathy to recognize that each member has a unique and valid perspective; and Discourse with students about contentious topics with appropriate supports and structures—and provides guidance and ideas about what this should look like in the classroom. Like most classroom practice, implementing the CUBED framework will require practice by both you and your students. Just as we do not expect our students to perfect their learning on the first try, it is important to anticipate what ongoing support and reflection looks like. Nothing we have presented to you is a guarantee for success. Rather we have focused more on having clear goals, planning ahead, and being prepared for when something goes wrong. There will be times that you fail and that is okay, because a FAIL is a First Attempt In Learning.

We have heard from many educators that they are worried about the fallout from students, families, and the community if they do "fail." We do not want educators to live in fear of failing; rather, we want you to anticipate the barriers to the best of your ability and set you and your students up for success, even though we know that it will not always be the result we intended. As Maya Angelou wrote in *I Know Why the Caged Bird Sings*, the goal is to be "hoping for the best, prepared for the worst, and unsurprised by anything in between." This is why we cannot stress enough the importance of working with your administration and communicating with your students and families. Bringing everyone together on the same page as often as you can will help to alleviate the potential for misunderstandings and related problems. There is not one correct teaching method that will prevent every upset phone call or tense email. Our experience tells us that while that may be unavoidable, bringing everyone along on your journey together will help to bridge the gaps needed to work through the hurt and angry feelings when something does go wrong.

Even once you have completed a review of your district curriculum or implemented new practices into your classroom, the work is always ongoing. See the "thousand-mile journey" as a positive instead of a negative. Do not worry that the work will never be done; rather, think of it as a way to provide countless opportunities to learn and improve. Each new day will bring new students, new topics, and new resources for everyone to think about. This is why curriculum and standards should always undergo periodic review so that they are always relevant and up to date. Ongoing review means that the changes come in small chunks on a regular basis instead of a "big change" all in one day. Do not forget the advice about how to eat an elephant: one bite at a time.

Lastly, educators know that just because a lesson worked one time does not mean it will work as well the next time. It may shift from class to class and is very likely to change from year to year, but planning ahead and continually reflecting on those plans allows the art of teaching to flourish. Give yourself the grace to accept that there will be ups and downs. Remember that teaching is often more of an art than a science. We hope that this book has given you the paint and brushes you need to work with any canvas you are presented with. Your dedication to this work, paired with the students who are allowed to share their true genius, is the blueprint to a masterpiece. No masterpiece has ever been easy, but we are here to tell you that it will be worth it. Your students, school, and community need you now, more than ever.

Keep having those conversations.

References

Adichie, C. N. (2009). The danger of a single story. *TED*. Retrieved October 13, 2021, from https://www.ted.com/talks/chimamanda_ngozi_adichie_the_danger_of_a_single_story

Albuquerque Public Schools. (n.d.). *Webb's depth of knowledge guide: Career and technical education definitions*. https://www.aps.edu/sapr/documents/resources/Webbs_DOK_Guide.pdf

American Historical Association. (2021, September). *Perspectives on History*. Retrieved October 13, 2021, from https://www.historians.org/publications-and-directories/perspectives-on-history/september-2021

Arizona State University. (2020, October 20). *The Civic Discourse Project: 'Civic Education and Renewal.'* https://azpbs.org/2020/10/the-civil-discourse-project-civic-education-and-renewal/

Arnold, K. (2013, October 11). What's the difference between dialogue and discussion? *The Extraordinary Team*. Retrieved October 14, 2021, from https://www.extraordinaryteam.com/dialogue_discussion/

ASCD. 2012. *What is the purpose of education?* Retrieved September 29, 2021, from https://ascd.org/ASCD/pdf/journals/ed_update/eu201207_infographic.pdf

Authentic Education. (2015). *What is Understanding by Design®?* Retrieved October 14, 2021, from https://www.authenticeducation.org/ubd/ubd.lasso

Barthel, M., Mitchell, A., & Holcomb, J. (2020, August 27). *Many Americans believe fake news is sowing confusion*. Pew Research Center Journalism Project. Retrieved October 14, 2021, from https://www.journalism.org/2016/12/15/many-americans-believe-fake-news-is-sowing-confusion/

Blackwood, K. (2020, October 5). Linguist links language to social change in 'words matter'. *Cornell Chronicle*. Retrieved October 14, 2021, from https://news.cornell.edu/stories/2020/10/linguist-links-language-social-change-words-matter

Bowen, R. S. (1970, June 10). *Understanding by Design*. Vanderbilt University Center for Teaching. Retrieved October 14, 2021, from https://cft.vanderbilt.edu/guides-sub-pages/understanding-by-design/

Brown Easton, L. (2015, April 1). *The art of dialogue*. ASCD. Retrieved October 14, 2021, from http://www.ascd.org/publications/educational-leadership/apr15/vol72/num07/The-Art-of-Dialogue.aspx

Bruce, G. (2021, April 20). *The greatest athlete of all time, according to Americans*. YouGovAmerica. https://today.yougov.com/topics/sports/articles-reports/2021/04/20/greatest-athlete-all-time-according-americans

Buffalo Games. *I dissent*. (2020). Retrieved October 14, 2021, from https://buffalogames.com/i-dissent/

Byford, J., Lennon, S., & Russell, W. B. (2009). Teaching controversial issues in the social studies: A research study of high school teachers. *The Clearing House: A Journal of Educational Strategies, Issues and Ideas*, *82*(4), 165–170.

Caffrey, G. (n.d.). *LETS ACT.* Retrieved October 14, 2021, from https://www.genevievecaffrey.com/lets-act.html

Chokshi, N. (2017, April 26). That wasn't Mark Twain: How a misquotation is born. *New York Times*. Retrieved October 14, 2021, from https://www.nytimes.com/2017/04/26/books/famous-misquotations.html

CIRCLE. (2020, November 25). *Election Week 2020: Young people increase turnout, lead Biden to victory*. Tufts University Center for Information and Research on Civic Learning and Engagement. Retrieved October 14, 2021, from https://circle.tufts.edu/latest-research/election-week-2020

CIRCLE. (2021). *Commission on Youth Voting and Civic Knowledge*. Tufts University Center for Information and Research on Civic Learning and Engagement. Retrieved October 14, 2021, from https://circle.tufts.edu/our-research/broadening-youth-voting/commission-youth-voting-and-civic-knowledge

Citizen University. (2021, October 5). *About Citizen University*. Retrieved October 13, 2021, from https://citizenuniversity.us/about/

Coloroso, B. (2010). *The bully, the bullied, and the bystander: From preschool to high school–How parents and teachers can help break the cycle*. HarperCollins.

Cullen, S., & Sharma, V. (n.d.). Short report on initial political polarization/argument visualization study. *PhilPapers*. Retrieved October 14, 2021, from https://philpapers.org/rec/CULSRO

David, S. (2017). The gift and power of emotional courage. *TEDWomen*. https://www.ted.com/talks/susan_david_the_gift_and_power_of_emotional_courage/transcript#t-1010427

Dewey, J. (1934). Individual psychology and education. *The Philosopher*, *12*(1), 1–6.

Dictionary.com. (2021). *Controversial: Definition & meaning*. Retrieved October 14, 2021, from https://www.dictionary.com/browse/controversial

Dimok, M., & Wike, R. (2020, November 13). America is exceptional in the nature of its political divide. *Pew Research Center*. https://www.pewresearch.org/fact-tank/2020/11/13/america-is-exceptional-in-the-nature-of-its-political-divide/

Drummond,M.(2015,December16).Politicsintheclassroom:Howmuchistoo much? *NPR*. https://www.npr.org/sections/ed/2015/12/16/459673575/politics-in-the-classroom-how-much-is-too-much

Duggan, M. (2017, July 11). *Online harassment 2017*. Pew Research Center: Internet, Science & Tech. Retrieved October 1, 2021, from https://www.pewresearch.org/internet/2017/07/11/online-harassment-2017/

Dusso, A., & Kennedy, S. S. (2015). Does ignorance matter? The relative importance of civic knowledge and the human tendency to engage in motivated reasoning. *Journal of Public and Nonprofit Affairs*, *1*(1), 59–72. https://doi.org/10.20899/jpna.1.1.59-72

EdSource. (2002, April). *The civic purposes of public schools*. Retrieved September 29, 2021, from https://edsource.org/wp-content/publications/CivicReport_Final.pdf

Elliott, E. (2018, August 20). Why read *Why Learn History* (when it's already summarized in this article)? *Perspectives on History*. https://www.historians.org/publications-and-directories/perspectives-on-history/september-2018/why-read-emwhy-learn-history/em-(when-its-already-summarized-in-this-article)

Facing History and Ourselves. (n.d.). *F.O.G. analysis*. Retrieved October 14, 2021, from https://www.facinghistory.org/chunk/fog-analysis

Facing History and Ourselves. (2021a). *Our approach*. Retrieved October 13, 2021, from https://www.facinghistory.org/our-approach

Facing History and Ourselves. (2021b). *Stolen lives: The Indigenous peoples of Canada and the Indian residential schools*. Retrieved October 13, 2021, from https://www.facinghistory.org/books-borrowing/stolen-lives-indigenous-peoples-canada-and-indian-residential-schools

Facing History and Ourselves. (2021c). Words matter. In *Holocaust and human behavior* (Chapter 1). Retrieved October 14, 2021, from https://www.facinghistory.org/holocaust-and-human-behavior/chapter-1/words-matter

Fairfax County Public Schools. (2014). *Portrait of a graduate*. https://www.fcps.edu/about-fcps/portrait-graduate

Fan, C. Y., & Chen, G. D. (2021). A scaffolding tool to assist learners in argumentative writing. *Computer Assisted Language Learning*, *34* (1–2), 159–183. https://doi.org/10.1080/09588221.2019.1660685

Finlay, L. (2008). *Reflecting on 'Reflective practice'*. Practice-Based Professional Learning Paper 52, The Open University. http://oro

.open.ac.uk/68945/1/Finlay-%282008%29-Reflecting-on-reflective-practice-PBPL-paper-52.pdf
Foshay, A. W. (1991). The curriculum matrix: Transcendence and mathematics. *Journal of Curriculum and Supervision*, 6(4), 277–293.
Fronius, T., Darling-Hammond, S., Persson, H., Guckenburg, S., Hurley, N., & Petrosino, A. (2019). *Restorative justice in US schools: An updated research review*. WestEd. https://www.wested.org/wp-content/uploads/2019/04/resource-restorative-justice-in-u-s-schools-an-updated-research-review.pdf
Garrett, H. J. (2019). Why does fake news work? On the psychosocial dynamics of learning, belief, and citizenship. In W. Journell (Ed.), *Unpacking fake news: An educator's guide to navigating the media with students* (pp. 15–29). Teachers College Press.
Gladstone, B. (2017). *The trouble with reality: A rumination on moral panic in our time*. Workman Publishing. Retrieved October 14, 2021, from https://www.workman.com/products/the-trouble-with-reality
Godin, S. (2009, August 23). Thanks for leading. *Seth's Blog*. Retrieved October 14, 2021, from https://seths.blog/2009/08/thanks-for-leading/
Gonzalez, J. (2015, October 15). *The big list of class discussion strategies*. Cult of Pedagogy. Retrieved October 14, 2021, from https://www.cultofpedagogy.com/speaking-listening-techniques/
Harrell, M. (2012). Assessing the efficacy of argument diagramming to teach critical thinking skills in introduction to philosophy. *Inquiry: Critical Thinking Across the Disciplines*, 27(2), 31–39. https://doi.org/10.5840/inquiryct201227210
Hastwell, C. (2020, December 23). The difference between debate, discussion and dialogue. *Great Place to Work*. Retrieved October 14, 2021, from https://www.greatplacetowork.com/resources/blog/the-difference-between-debate-discussion-and-dialogue
Hess, D. E. (2009). *Controversy in the classroom: The democratic power of discussion*. Routledge.
Hess, D. E., & McAvoy, P. (2014). *The political classroom: Evidence and ethics in democratic education*. Routledge.
Ho, L., McAvoy, P., Hess, D., & Gibbs, B. (2017). Teaching and learning about controversial issues and topics in the social studies. In M. M. Manfra & C. M. Bolick (Eds.), *Wiley handbook of social studies research* (pp. 319–335). Wiley.
Humphries, E. (2020, December 1). Teachers need support as they wade into the 2020 election. *The Hechinger Report*. Retrieved October 14, 2021, from https://hechingerreport.org/opinion-our-schools-must-figure-out-a-way-to-teach-this-presidential-election/
Indian Prairie School District 204. (n.d.). *Comparison of dialogue and debate*. https://ipsdweb.ipsd.org/uploads/PDAC/ComparisonofDialogueandDebate_0310.pdf

Infobase. (n.d.). *Issues & controversies*. Retrieved October 14, 2021, from https://www.infobase.com/product/schools/issues-controversies-online-2/

Jensen, A., Marble, W., Scheve, K., & Slaughter, M. J. (2021). City limits to partisan polarization in the American public. *Political Science Research and Methods*, *9*(2), 223–241.

Johnson, D. W., & Johnson, R. T. (1988). Critical thinking through structured controversy. *Educational Leadership*, *45*(8), 58–64.

Johnson, D. W., & Johnson, R. T. (1993). Creative and critical thinking through academic controversy. *American Behavioral Scientist*, *37*(1), 40–53. https://doi.org/10.1177%2F0002764293037001005

Jones, R., Jr. [@SonofBaldwin] (2015, August 15). We can disagree and still love each other unless your disagreement is rooted in my oppression and denial of my humanity and right to exist [Tweet]. *Twitter*. https://twitter.com/SonofBaldwin/status/633644373423562753?s=20

Journell, W. (2016). Teacher political disclosure as parrhēsia. *Teachers College Record*, *118*(5), 1–36. https://doi.org/10.1177%2F016146811611800508

Journell, W. (2021a). Exacerbating existing divides: Fake news, desire, and partisanship. In G. L. Samuels and A. Samuels (Eds.), *The divide within: Intersections of realities, facts, theories, and practices* (pp. 15–38). Information Age Publishing.

Journell, W. (2021b). Taking a reasoned stance against misinformation. *Phi Delta Kappan*, *102*(5), 12–17. https://doi.org/10.1177%2F0031721721992559

Kawashima-Ginsberg, K. (2013, April). *Do discussion, debate, and simulations boost NAEP civics performance?* Tufts University Center for Information and Research on Civic Learning and Engagement. Retrieved October 14, 2021, from https://circle.tufts.edu/sites/default/files/2020-01/discussion_debate_naep_2013.pdf

Killough, A. (2021, October 16). Texas school administrator told teachers to include Holocaust books with 'opposing' views when explaining new state law. *CNN*. https://www.cnn.com/2021/10/15/us/texas-schools-books-holocaust-state-law/index.html

King, L. J., Vickery, A. E., & Caffrey, G. (2018). A pathway to racial literacy: Using the LETS ACT Framework to teach controversial issues. *Social Education*, *82*(6), 316–322. Retrieved October 14, 2021, from https://www.socialstudies.org/social-education/82/6/pathway-racial-literacy-using-lets-act-framework-teach-controversial-issues

Knowledge Matters Campaign. (2018). *It's time for a reading reset!* Retrieved October 14, 2021, from https://knowledgematterscampaign.org/wp-content/uploads/2018/04/KMC-Announcement-re-2018-NAEP-v2.pdf

Kwan, V. (2019). Responsible reporting in an age of information disorder. *First Draft*. Retrieved October 14, 2021, from https://firstdraftnews.org/wp-content/uploads/2019/10/Responsible_Reporting_Digital_AW-1.pdf

Laursen, B., & Collins, W. A. (2009). Parent-child relationships during adolescence. In R. M. Lerner & L. Steinberg (Eds.), *Handbook of adolescent psychology: Contextual influences on adolescent development* (pp. 3–42). John Wiley & Sons, Inc. https://doi.org/10.1002/9780470479193.adlpsy002002

Lesh, B. (2011). *Why won't you just tell us the answer?* Stenhouse Publishers.

Levine, P. (2013). *We are the ones we have been waiting for.* Oxford University Press.

Levine, P. (2014, July 24). Frontiers of Democracy 2014—Peter Levine, Tisch College. *YouTube*. https://youtu.be/txjYVUqNCik

Liu, E. (2019). How to revive your belief in democracy. *TED*. Retrieved October 13, 2021, from https://www.ted.com/talks/eric_liu_how_to_revive_your_belief_in_democracy?language=en

Lorde, A. (1984). *Sister outsider: Essays and speeches*. Crossing Press.

Lutz Fernandez, A. (2021, August 23). School Covid mask rules have sparked parent-teacher violence. We can't ignore it. *NBC News THINK*. https://www.nbcnews.com/think/opinion/school-covid-mask-rules-have-sparked-parent-teacher-violence-we-ncna1277415

Mann, H. (1848). *Report no. 12 of the Massachusetts School Board*. Retrieved September 29, 2021, from https://usa.usembassy.de/etexts/democrac/16.htm

Marzano, R. (2004). The importance of background knowledge. In *Building background knowledge for academic achievement: Research on what works in schools*. ASCD. Retrieved October 14, 2021, from http://www.ascd.org/publications/books/104017/chapters/The-Importance-of-Background-Knowledge.aspx

Massachusetts Council for the Social Studies. (2018). *49th Annual Northeast Regional Conference for the Social Studies*. https://www.masscouncil.org/?page_id=6383#

McAvoy, P., & McAvoy, G. E. (2021). Can debate and deliberation reduce partisan divisions? evidence from a study of high school students. *Peabody Journal of Education*, *96*(3), 275–284. https://doi.org/10.1080/0161956x.2021.1942706

McConnell-Ginet, S. (2020). *Words matter: Meaning and power*. Cambridge University Press.

McManus, J. H. (2012). *Detecting bull: How to identify bias and junk journalism in print, broadcast and on the wild web*. Unvarnished Press.

McTighe, J., & Wiggins, G. (1998). *Understanding by Design*. ASCD.

Merriam-Webster. (2021a). *Merriam-Webster dictionary*. https://www.merriam-webster.com/dictionary/

Merriam-Webster. (2021b). *Contentious*. Retrieved October 14, 2021, from https://www.merriam-webster.com/dictionary/contentious#synonyms

Merriam-Webster. (2021c). *Controversial*. Retrieved October 14, 2021, from https://www.merriam-webster.com/dictionary/controversial#synonyms

Merriam-Webster. (2021d). *Debate*. Retrieved October 14, 2021, from https://www.merriam-webster.com/dictionary/debate

Merriam-Webster. (2021e). *Disinformation*. Retrieved October 14, 2021, from https://www.merriam-webster.com/dictionary/disinformation

Metropolitan State University of Denver. (2008). *MSU Denver academic misconduct process*. Retrieved October 14, 2021, from https://temp.msudenver.edu/media/content/deanofstudents/conflictresolution/MSUDenverAcademicMisconductProcess.pdf

Nathan, E., & Lee, C. K. E. (2004). Using structured academic controversies in the social studies classroom. *Teaching and Learning*, *25*(2), 171–188. http://hdl.handle.net/10497/336

National Council for the Social Studies. (n.d.). *3 steps to civil discourse in the classroom*. Retrieved October 14, 2021, from https://www.socialstudies.org/sites/default/files/3_steps_to_civil_discourse_teacher_version_1.pdf

National Council for the Social Studies. (2010). *National curriculum standards for social studies: Executive summary*. https://www.socialstudies.org/standards/national-curriculum-standards-social-studies-executive-summary

National Council for the Social Studies. (2017). *College, Career, and Civic Life (C3) Framework for Social Studies State Standards: Guidance for enhancing the rigor of K-12 civics, economics, geography, and history*. Retrieved October 14, 2021, from https://www.socialstudies.org/standards/c3

National Council for the Social Studies. (2018). *College, Career, & Civic Life (C3) survey results*. Retrieved September 29, 2021, from https://www.socialstudies.org/sites/default/files/tssp_announcements/c3_survey_results.pdf

National Museum of the American Indian. (2018). *Native knowledge: Words matter case study*. https://americanindian.si.edu/nk360/plains-treaties/words-matter

North, R. (2003, June 26). *Healing the scars of war in Sierra Leone*. International Federation of Red Cross And Red Crescent Societies. https://reliefweb.int/report/sierra-leone/healing-scars-war-sierra-leone

O'Reilly, T., Wang, Z., & Sabatini, J. (2019). How much knowledge is too little? When a lack of knowledge becomes a barrier to comprehension. *Psychological Science*, *30*(9), 1344–1351. https://doi.org/10.1177%2F0956797619862276

Oxford Languages. (2021a). *Or*. Google English Dictionary. Retrieved October 14, 2021, from https://www.google.com

Oxford Languages. (2021b). *Versus*. Google English Dictionary. Retrieved October 14, 2021, from https://www.google.com

Parker, W. C. (2010). Listening to strangers: Classroom discussion in democratic education. *Teachers College Record*, *112*(11), 2815–2832.

Peace Corps. (n.d.). *The blind men and the elephant.* Retrieved October 13, 2021, from https://www.peacecorps.gov/educators/resources/story-blind-men-and-elephant/

Pew Research Center. (2016, June 27). *On views of race and inequality, Blacks and Whites are worlds apart.* https://www.pewresearch.org/social-trends/2016/06/27/on-views-of-race-and-inequality-blacks-and-whites-are-worlds-apart/

ProCon.org. (2021, September 28). *ProCon.org website.* Retrieved October 14, 2021, from https://www.procon.org/

Putnam, R. D. (2000). *Bowling alone: The collapse and revival of American community.* Simon & Schuster.

Quinn, F.M. (1998) Reflection and reflective practice. In F. M. Quinn (ed.), *Continuing professional development in nursing.* Stanley Thornes.

Quote Investigator. (2014). *A lie can travel halfway around the world while the truth is putting on its shoes.* Retrieved October 14, 2021, from https://quoteinvestigator.com/2014/07/13/truth/

Restrepo, S. (2019). *Brené Brown: The call to courage* [Film]. Netflix.

Right Question Institute. (2021, September 30). *What is the QFT?* Retrieved October 14, 2021, from https://rightquestion.org/what-is-the-qft/

Schaps, E., Schaeffer, E. F., & McDonnell, S. N. (2001). What's right and wrong in character education today. *Education Week, 21*(2), 40–44.

Schmidt, J. (2020, October 4). *Preparing to talk about the Election.* https://joeschmidtsocialstudies.com/blog/f/preparing-to-talk-about-the-election

Segall, A., Crocco, M. S., Halvorson, A., & Jacobsen, R. (2019). Teaching in the twilight zone of misinformation, disinformation, alternative facts, and fake news. In W. Journell (Ed.), *Unpacking fake news: An educator's guide to navigating the media with students* (pp. 74–91). Teachers College Press.

Shonk, K. (2019, May 27). Conflict resolution examples in history: Learning from nuclear disarmament. *Harvard Law School Program on Negotiation Daily Blog.* https://www.pon.harvard.edu/daily/conflict-resolution/conflict-resolution-examples-in-history-learning-from-nuclear-disarmament/

Smith, M. (2011a, June 14). None of us is as smart as all of us. *Marketing Eye.* https://www.marketingeye.com.au/marketing-blog/management/none-of-us-is-as-smart-as-all-of-us.html

Southern Poverty Law Center. (2016, April 13). *SPLC survey: Presidential campaign leading to widespread fear, bullying in schools.* Retrieved October 14, 2021, from https://www.splcenter.org/news/2016/04/13/splc-survey-presidential-campaign-leading-widespread-fear-bullying-schools

St. Petersburg—USA Orphanage Research Team. (2008). The effects of early social-emotional and relationship experience on the development of young orphanage children. *Monographs of the Society for Research in Child Development*, *73*(3), vii. https://dx.doi.org/10.1111%2Fj.1540-5834.2008.00483.x

Stanford History Education Group. (2019, November 14). *Students' civic online reasoning: A national portrait.* https://cor.stanford.edu/research/students-civic-online-reasoning-a-national-portrait-2021/

Stanford History Education Group. (2020, June 23). *Historical thinking chart.* https://sheg.stanford.edu/history-lessons/historical-thinking-chart

Steele, L. (2021, May 20). Playing for peace: How basketball is building bridges across the sectarian divide in Northern Ireland, with around 90% of schools still segregated by religion. *Daily Mail.* https://www.dailymail.co.uk/sport/othersports/article-9600223/How-basketball-building-bridges-sectarian-divide-Northern-Ireland.html

Stern, J., & Aleo, T. (2020, September 9). Conceptually speaking: Ayo Magwood talks inequity, antiracism, and history. *Buzzsprout.* Retrieved October 13, 2021, from https://conceptuallyspeaking.buzzsprout.com/1073776/5364550-ayo-magwood-talks-inequity-antiracism-and-history

Stern, J., Ferraro, K., Duncan, K., & Aleo, T. (2021). *Learning that transfers: Designing curriculum for a changing world.* Corwin.

Street Law Inc. (2021). *Deliberations.* Retrieved October 14, 2021, from https://store.streetlaw.org/deliberations/?page=3

Stunson, M. (2021, April 14). Teacher who used racial slur next to Tupac photo put on administrative leave in Texas. *Kansas City Star.* https://www.kansascity.com/news/nation-world/national/article250664139.html

ThinkerAnalytix. (2021). *About argument mapping.* Retrieved October 14, 2021, from https://thinkeranalytix.org/about-argument-mapping/

Tuckman, B. W. (1965). Developmental sequence in small groups. *Psychological Bulletin*, *63*(6), 384–399. https://doi.org/10.1037/h0022100

U.S. Courts. (n.d.). *Setting ground rules: Civil discourse and difficult decisions.* Retrieved October 14, 2021, from https://www.uscourts.gov/educational-resources/educational-activities/setting-ground-rules-civil-discourse-and-difficult

Underwood, J. (2017, December 4). Under the law: School districts control teachers' classroom speech. *Phi Delta Kappan*, *99*(4), 76–77. http://kappanonline.org/underwood-school-districts-control-teachers-classroom-speech/

Van Benthuysen, H., & Hodgin, E. Talking across political differences. *Educator Innovator.* (2019, March 19). Retrieved October 14, 2021, from https://educatorinnovator.org/talking-across-political-differences/

van der Brugge, E. (2018). *The use of argument mapping in improving critical thinking* [PhD thesis, University of Melbourne]. http://hdl.handle.net/11343/214519

van Woerkom, M. (2018, March 12). *Building community with restorative circles*. Edutopia. Retrieved October 14, 2021, from https://www.edutopia.org/article/building-community-restorative-circles

Visions of Education. (2020, June 4). *Episode 100: Teaching racial literacy and controversial issues with Genevieve Caffrey*. Retrieved October 14, 2021, from https://visionsofed.com/2019/01/01/episode-100-teaching-racial-literacy-and-controversial-issues-with-genevieve-caffrey/

Vygotsky, L. (1978). *Mind in society: The development of higher psychological processes*. Harvard University Press.

Wagner, T. (1993, September). Systemic change: Rethinking the purpose of school. *Educational Leadership*. *51*(1), 24–28. http://www1.ascd.org/publications/educational-leadership/sept93/vol51/num01/Systemic-Change@-Rethinking-the-Purpose-of-School.aspx

Walsh, J. A., & Sattes, B. D. (2016). Prepare the question: What are the distinguishing features of quality questions? In *Quality questioning: Research-based practice to engage every learner* (pp. 58–65). Corwin.

Wang, J. (2001). Orientation day. In V. Nam (Ed.), *YELL-oh girls! Emerging voices explore culture, identity, and growing up Asian American* (pp. 199–200). HarperCollins.

Wardle, C. (2019, October). Understanding information disorder. *First Draft*. https://firstdraftnews.org/wp-content/uploads/2019/10/Information_Disorder_Digital_AW.pdf?x32994

Watson, A. (2020, October 12). Online sharing of fake news U.S. 2019. *Statista*. Retrieved October 14, 2021, from https://www.statista.com/statistics/657111/fake-news-sharing-online/.=

Weedon, J., Nuland, W., & Stamos, A. (2017). *Information operations and Facebook*. https://i2.res.24o.it/pdf2010/Editrice/ILSOLE24ORE/ILSOLE24ORE/Online/_Oggetti_Embedded/Documenti/2017/04/28/facebook-and-information-operations-v1.pdf

Wellman, B., & Lipton, L. (2017). *Data-driven dialogue: A facilitator's guide to collaborative inquiry* (2nd ed.). Mira Via LLC.

Williams, J. (2021, June 14). GOP preparing the ground to steal an election. *The Hill*. Retrieved October 14, 2021, from https://www.msn.com/en-us/news/politics/juan-williams-gop-preparing-the-ground-to-steal-an-election/ar-AAL1fUx

Wineburg, S. (2010, Winter). Thinking like a historian. *Teaching With Primary Sources Quarterly*, *3*(1), 2–4.

Wineburg, S. (2015). *Why historical thinking is not about history*. Retrieved October 13, 2021, from https://stacks.stanford.edu/file/druid:yy383km0067/Wineburg%20Hist.%20Thinking%20is%20not%20about%20history.pdf

Wineburg, S., McGrew, S., Breakstone, J., & Ortega, T. (2016). *Evaluating information: The cornerstone of civic online reasoning*. Stanford History Education Group. Retrieved October 14, 2021, from

https://stacks.stanford.edu/file/druid:fv751yt5934/SHEG%20 Evaluating%20Information%20Online.pdf
Wisconsin Center for Education Research. (2017a). *Teacher moves: Facilitate student reasoning and collaboration.* http://stem4els.wceruw.org/How/teacher.html
Wisconsin Center for Education Research. (2017b). *Student moves: Teach the language of complex thinking.* http://stem4els.wceruw.org/How/student.html
Wong, H. K., & Wong, R. T. (1997). *The first days of school: How to be an effective teacher.* Wong Publications.
Zimmerman, J. (2005). *Whose America? Culture wars in the public schools.* Harvard University Press.

Index

Clear Flog: Facts, Opinions or generalization